Children dance
in the classroom

Children dance in the classroom

BY *Geraldine Dimondstein*
UNIVERSITY EXTENSION,
THE UNIVERSITY OF CALIFORNIA,
LOS ANGELES

The Macmillan Company
NEW YORK
Collier-Macmillan Limited
LONDON

THE MACMILLAN COMPANY
866 Third Avenue, New York, New York 10022
Collier-Macmillan Canada, Ltd., Toronto, Ontario
Library of Congress catalog card number: 74–134885
FIRST PRINTING

Foreword

CHILDREN DANCE IN THE CLASSROOM *is an entirely fresh approach not duplicated in any book in print today. It is my opinion that this volume will have a tremendous import not only in the area of dance but also in education and the behavioral sciences.*

The conceptual framework is so magnificently defined that there is no current book in the field that can measure up to it. It is moving in the direction of the forethought in all the behavioral sciences. The interrelationship of ideas and the implementation of them present a comprehensive viewpoint in a practical, workable, and exciting framework.

I am particularly impressed with two major tenets which carry through the entire book—that of focusing on expression in the child's environment and that observation is an overt form of experience which extends the creative imagination of children. Dr. Dimondstein's examples and suggested approaches to classroom dance are clearly defined. Her criticisms of practice in rhythmic and dance education in the elementary schools are both timely and cogent.

Dr. Dimondstein is not only a lucid writer but her rich background in the arts, music and movement has given her the capacity to write with authority.

VALERIE V. HUNT
Professor of Physical Education
UCLA

Preface

This book has come into being in the belief that one of the
major functions of elementary schooling is to develop in
children a sense of self-knowledge and self-identification
with their own creative abilities. A child's knowledge of
himself and his environment is deepened by his involvement
in the qualitative aspects of experience, and participation in
the arts enhances such awareness. Dance, as one form, allows
a child to know himself in still another way, through the
body's capacity to express feelings through the forms of
movement. For this reason dance belongs in the classroom.

The materials presented here have evolved over a period
of twenty years of teaching music and movement to children
in nursery and elementary schools and of introducing concepts
of dance to students and teachers where they were frequently
omitted in programs of teacher education. Some of the actual
classroom problems are elaborations of an experimental
development project in the arts and humanities for young
children. The content and format of the lessons represent a
synthesis of children's explorations in diverse educational
environments and are suggested as a working model for
teachers. Because it is difficult to "talk" dance and even more
difficult to interpret it from the written word, the intent is
to provide a form which unifies underlying concepts and
instructional procedures and at the same time allows for the
unpredictable responses from teachers and children that will
emerge from the discovery process.

Because movement comes into being only through the combined use of space–time–force, there is no objectively defined beginning. As the structure of the conceptual framework, each of these concepts is described in a separate section in terms of its distinguishing characteristics and related dance elements. In any concept a teacher will find that she is incorporating elements from other concepts, in keeping with the problems posed by the children. Lessons are extensions of the concepts and are designed as open-ended experiences which allow for as many solutions as there are children in the group. They are of indeterminate time and are not necessarily intended to "fit" into one class period. Rather, each lesson offers a wide range of explorations and contains enough material for many sessions. Ultimately the sensitivity of the teacher and the responsiveness of the children will determine together how far a problem can be developed.

Lessons are presented as creative dance problems, which move from those with simple solutions to those requiring increasing levels of sophistication. This simply means that a teacher may explore a problem for herself, or with a first or fifth grader, and that each brings to it increasing levels of sophistication, not in terms of technical polish, but in terms of expressive forms. As a broad definition, creative problem solving is an approach which seeks to integrate the learning of skills with the expression of qualities of movement. If a child lacks a specific skill in executing a particular movement, it is at that point that he senses a need for technique and may be made aware of alternatives. When a child is unable to reconcile his ability with his intentions, as frequently happens, he can be guided into problems which reinforce his ability to seek new solutions. Skills, then, become the subjective grappling of the elements of movement that are necessary to objectify or symbolize a child's need for expressive dance forms.

A problem-solving approach serves two important functions in the teaching–learning situation: it frees a child to discover his own problems within a given context, and it releases the teacher from being overly directive, by allowing her to make guided observations and reserve judgments while the process is in motion. It is hoped that presenting materials in this way will offer teachers a conceptual framework with suggested learning experiences which permit them to move comfortably into their own improvisations. Each lesson, therefore, is designed to include both concepts and movement elements within the following structure.

I. Concept

SPACE *direction, level, path, range, body shape, body parts.*
TIME *rhythmic and metrical; beat, accent, measure, phrasing.*
FORCE *sustained, percussive, swinging, vibratory.*

II. Problem

Exploration of a concept using related movement elements in various types of contexts.

SOLUTIONS *Observed movements of children. Solutions will not be noted for each problem; personalized responses will serve as examples of the infinite movement possibilities.*

III. Problem

Extensions or elaborations of the initial problem; ideas may emerge from the children or are suggested by the teachers.

ADDITIONAL ELEMENTS *Elements drawn from other concepts that are used to elaborate the problem.*

There is no delineation of movement experiences in terms of grade levels because the arts, perhaps more than any other area, lend themselves to a nongraded approach. Because there is no prescribed sequential development in the art process other than the maturational limitations of a child at any given time, there should be no rigorous ordering of a child's abilities and attainments into a graded structure. By the same token, notions of "typicality" associated with a graded system have even less meaning for the arts than for other disciplines. Because expression in dance is predominantly idiomatic, it is the child who establishes the order of his own content in relation to what he is able to perceive and produce.

Each dance session is designed to help teachers develop a kinesthetic awareness of movement possibilities, as well as a verbal vocabulary which communicates directly to children. Although in many cases the dialogue does not specify repetition or the need for the further development of a given problem, each teacher must draw from her immediate experience with the children to determine whether such may be desirable. Ideas are expressed in dance terms so that the "doing" and the "meaning" are immediately related to the body in motion. This approach to a creative dance program is intended for potential elementary classroom teachers, practicing elementary and preschool teachers, and private teachers of dance to young children. Although it is essentially designed for the nonspecialist teacher, it may offer useful insights for dance specialists as well. In all situations the purpose is to make dance both a "knowing" and a "doing" experience, and to help children express themselves through another language, that of dance movement.

G. D.

Acknowledgments

To those who have been closest and most responsive to the directions that I have been pursuing in pressing for the importance of dance in the education of young children, I express my gratitude:

NAIMA PREVOTS, *Professor of Dance, American University, colleague and friend, who in a fruitful year of working together on a curriculum and film in children's dance has been of invaluable assistance in helping me to elaborate my ideas. My thanks also for her painstaking efforts in reading the manuscript.*

FREDA MADDOW, *who brought her experience as a Graham dancer, for her careful scrutiny and suggestions while reading the chapters in the course of their preparation.*

JACQUELINE PAUL *of New York, who took the photos of public school children in kindergarten through third grades in Washington and Virginia, and* CLEO TRUMBO, *who photographed the children in the fourth, fifth, and sixth grades at the Westland School in Los Angeles—both sensitive photographers and close friends; their photographic descriptions give life to the written word.*

And above all, VALERIE HUNT, *Professor of Physical Education at UCLA, whose scholarly research into the sources of movement behavior most profoundly influenced my formulation of a conceptual framework for dance in education. I am deeply grateful for her intellectual and moral support in the reading of this manuscript.*

G. D.

Contents

IV

Expressive movement through imagery

V

Dance as knowing, doing, and valuing

VI

Resources

I

Dance as knowing and feeling

1. *Dance as creative expression*

Dance is one of the primary forms of human expression. Historically, it has served many functions in society, ranging from group ritual and spectacle to individual expression of ideas, feelings, and emotions. Some of the most sublime and creative works of man in the twentieth century have been expressed through dance, both in Europe, with ballet or classical dance, and in the United States, with what has been called modern dance. It is the latter which has greatly influenced the building of a tradition in dance, but its greatest contribution has been in giving dance to the individual. As an art form, it has broken away from the orthodoxy of traditional ballet and has given authenticity to personal expression.

For young children, especially those in elementary school, *dance* is defined as the interpretation of a child's ideas, feelings, and sensory impressions expressed symbolically in movement forms through the unique use of his body. Because each individual differs, it is especially fitting that we draw upon the forms of modern dance for movement experiences in the classroom in the sense of a continuous, open-ended search for an individual vocabulary. Experiences in dance are fundamental and accessible to all children because a child's body and its expression are one. It has

been said that to move is to be revealed for what we are. This means that the body is not an external instrument or a "thing" which a child manipulates. It is his very self, in that psychologically and kinesthetically it is a direct agent of his feelings. It is manipulated by a child through his need for expression, not as an instrument that is foreign to or outside of himself. It does not require mastery over a new instrument, but is an experience which involves the body completely. Thus, in bringing his own body under control, he controls the most immediate part of himself.

Studies from psychology and kinesiology tend to support the belief that from an activity point of view, movement is basic in children's learning. It may even be that movement is the initial way in which a child begins the creative process, and that within an appropriate educational setting, he may be inspired to release that creative potential through dance. No one can determine the extent of children's imaginative or creative abilities. Children know about rhythm because they have already experienced it in their everyday movements. They have yet to discover creative rhythmic movements, however, by learning ways in which they can use their bodies for creative expression. To do this

3

I: Dance as knowing and feeling

they must have actual experiences in being *consciously rhythmical*.[1]

Educational dance has its origin in the classroom and must be made available to all children as an inherent part of the educational process. Although dance is not "subject matter" in the traditional sense, there is a mode of knowledge to be learned. The end product is not more facts about the objective world, but deeper feelings about the self. The "subject" in this case is the individual, and the "matter" is the education of feelings and the development of sensibility expressed through movement forms. As such, every child can and should participate in the dance program, not simply the talented or gifted.

Although we are concerned with the basic elements of dance, the intent is not to produce dancers in the sense that years of study and intense training make the professional. Young children are in the exploratory stages of this art form and should not be led into dance expertness which might necessitate an undue emphasis upon technique. Rather, each child needs to experience a variety and range of movements in order to develop a dance vocabulary which bears his own imprint.

The whole process is ultimately more important than the specific activities within it. Creative innovation is manifested in degrees rather than by steps. There are degrees of awareness, sensitivity, and coordination involved in each child's movement. Through dance a child may show how he feels about people, objects, phenomena. Because of the strong social needs which operate, dance represents one form of communication through which a child shares his ideas and feelings with others. Although the creative process is manifestly an individualized effort, children gain rich experiences when they are able to share with one another.

Educational dance is also concerned with control of the body that differs from sports or gymnastics. Although learning to control one's body is the basis of all motor activity, creative movement is not task oriented in the same way. Both involve problem solving, but perception in dance is not geared toward the refinement of skills as ends in themselves. Rather, particular skills that are needed develop intrinsically as means and function to enhance a child's perception. The mastery of skills alone does not guarantee that dance is creative, but they are necessary

[1] Geraldine Dimondstein, *A Conceptual Model of the Arts as Sensuous Expression in the Education of Young Children*, unpublished dissertation. UCLA, 1967, p. 76.

4

as instruments which serve the expression of movement. The focus is on helping children develop perceptions that are essentially aesthetic, by encouraging them to respond to the qualitative, sensuous aspects of the dance experience.

Thus, the importance of a program in dance for children is to help them develop a kinesthetic awareness of their ability to use their bodies expressively. *Kinesthetic awareness* refers not only to a child's bodily reactions or muscle memory, but to a conscious perception of his body's ability to "feel" movement. Because dance is an art form and is not simply a physical activity, the perception must be aesthetic. This awareness is made perceptible through his senses and involves him in the total process of perceiving, feeling, and expressing.

As an art form, dance has a twofold purpose, communion with self and communication with others. It communicates through forms which are nondiscursive but speaks through movement. The essence of creative movement lies in examining the differences between those real-life gestures and those created in dance.

Suzanne Langer discusses dance as a mature art form, yet the same principles that she uses to define and clarify this form apply to an understanding of chil-dren's movement. Langer attributes much of the confusion as to what dance is to the fact that "its space is plastic, its time musical, its themes are fantasy, its actions symbolic. . . . Dance has been called an art of space, an art of time, a kind of po-etry . . . but it is none of these things." [2] Although these are supportive elements and are primary in other arts, they do not point to the essential illusion of dance which, she asserts, is the nature of ges-ture.

With adults as with children, dance finds its image through gestures that are not real, but that are created and shaped. Thus, it is not a purely visual art like painting, it is not plastic in the same sense as sculpture, nor is the presentation of fantasy the same as that in poetry. Its similarity to other arts is that feelings and ideas are expressed in symbolic form. Its distinctive characteristic is that it is a kinesthetic–visual image made tangible by means of the body.

Although all gestures are important in that they reflect personal experience, tem-perament, and emotional moods, all ges-tures that occur in daily living are not art. In children's normal activities, gestures

2 Suzanne Langer, *Feeling and Form* (New York: Charles Scribner's Sons, 1953), p. 204.

5

are used to convey intentions, desires, expectations, and they are spontaneous. An up-and-down wave of the hand, for example, is conventionally understood as "good-bye," just as a yawn is interpreted as a sign of fatigue or boredom. Within the realm of general behavior, gestures become an aspect of *self-expression* in the sense that they are immediately reflective of how a child feels at the moment. They may be random or uncontrolled, and are part of general, emotional experience. Gestures are transformed into dance movement, however, only when they are executed apart from the momentary situation or emotional impulse which prompted them. They then become responses evoked by emotions in relation to aesthetic elements, in this case, to space–time–force, which are explored for their qualitative, emotional dimensions.

A child in a fit of rage, for example, who flails his arms and legs in striking, slashing gestures is giving *vent* to self-expression, but a child who uses these gestures in relation to a defined movement problem is giving *form* to his expression. In the latter, he transmutes his emotions through the forms of movement and is giving expression not only to feeling but to the experience of that feeling. Dance gestures develop according to their own

logical demands. They do not follow the same changes in intensity, duration, or sequence as the actual feelings from which they emerge. They are abstracted from a whole range of feelings and are created and presented as forms which take on a life of their own.

The value of dance as an art, therefore, is in helping children achieve an awareness of the importance of organizing their emotions and of communicating them through the forms of movement. Because children express their emotions honestly and directly, they do not respond in depth when they are called upon to "pretend" to be something. It is not "pretending" which inspires movement; it is a sense of being. At the same time, creative movement does not emerge from real emotional states, but from remembered or imagined feelings. This is because the form of a particular feeling in everyday life is never experienced completely except as a memory, for it never exists fully at one time. If, for example, a child wishes to convey a mood of loneliness or solitude and he actually feels psychologically desolate, it is unlikely that he could give objective expression to that feeling. On the other hand, a teacher in setting a mood situation might suggest that he *imagine* that all his friends have wandered off and left him alone. At this moment, he may recall an emotion he has experienced before, and will react to that emotion in searching for expressive movements.

Similarly, emphasizing the expression of a movement quality rather than a literal idea points to the nature of emotion in dance. If a problem is presented of responding to physical elements in the environment, for example, a child may choose to explore the harmful effects of smog on living things in nature. Although he himself does not feel destructive or suffocating, he has presumably experienced how smog feels, smells, and looks. Through his selection of movement elements, his gestures will project qualities of weight, denseness, closeness, or whatever qualities capture the feeling of this amorphous entity. He knows he is not smog and he knows he is not pretending. Rather, he is directly engaged in expressing the qualities he has experienced in formulated movement terms. In so doing, his response to that experience is individual and symbolic, and the movements take on their own identity.

Whether dance problems involve emotional states, themes, or fragments of ideas, the common thread inherent in the making of symbolic form is *abstraction*.

It is this which differentiates between *self-expression* and an *aesthetic response*—in this case, between realistic and dance gestures. Dance does not derive its meanings from literal interpretations, nor does it communicate through conventional movements. It derives from feelings which children abstract from their everyday lives, and upon which they draw to present symbolically.

If, for example, in an exploration of body shape, a child were asked, "How small can you be? his choice of movements would be an abstraction of all the experiences he has had with "smallness," within the range of his body control. Because expressing smallness or any other quality can never show all his experiences at once, his choice of movements requires both synthesis and abstraction. In the process of exploration he must select and simplify significant elements from his experience to find ways of objectifying them in movement.

It is through creative problem solving that this process comes into being. A child is solving problems when he searches for ways that are new for him, at any point in his development. It is not important that a movement has been done before, nor does the fact of its novelty assure that it is especially successful or creative.

What is significant is that it is a new discovery for that child and that it becomes part of the process of selection and abstraction which he relates to his everchanging needs for expression.

As a key to understanding this phenomenon, teachers must accept the concept of *process*. This is not an artificial dichotomy between process and product, for they are closely related in any artistic endeavor. Rather, it is an awareness that aesthetic perception does not come about simply in making a piece of art, such as painting a picture, composing a poem, or moving rhythmically across the floor. It also emerges from a sensibility to the relationship of the elements in the experience through which the product is created and given meaning. It requires time for dance experiences to be internalized by a child, for in the process he must become consciously aware of what he has done, and of the elements involved.

Developing a sense of kinesthetic awareness makes it possible for a child to go beyond the mere "making" of a movement, to a consciousness of how and why it takes form. In this way, he begins to perceive the relationship between the body and its capacity for expression. The value of this approach is that it always permits experimentation from both the teacher and the child, with the everpresent realization that there may be other alternatives.

Although problem solving is descriptive of a mode of investigation, there are qualitative levels of performance within it. In relation to educational dance, these may range from *exploration* and *improvisation* to *dance study*. As this program is designed for children, experiences are designated as *explorations*, which imply a kind of sensing and experimenting with what the body can do in its encounter with dance elements. Initial explorations may be random, as a child literally "feels his way" in testing what the muscles can do and how he can bring his body under control. Exploring movement fundamentals serves as an example. Locomotor (walking, running, leaping, skipping, crawling) and nonlocomotor movement (swinging, rocking, swaying, bending) must be experienced by all children because they are basic to the development of more complicated patterns. Although such activities are presented to the entire group, each child explores them in his own manner, "educating" his muscles in ways that are unique to him.

Although there is no precise division, and no specific sequence in terms of time, exploration leads to improvision. *Improvi-*

sation comes into being only in the doing and is a continuous search for forms which emerge, recur, take on new dimensions, and may or may not be repeated. For most children development follows a back-and-forth, zigzag pattern, depending upon the nature of the problem. Improvisation usually moves beyond exploration in that it may not arise from random, fragmented ideas, but from within the structure of a problem which a child may define for himself.

Improvisational movements may be built around a concept, an element, or a specific image. For example, a problem of sensing accented beats may be elaborated through the imagery of clocks. Once they have explored the concept that rhythm is defined by accented and unaccented beats, children may select clocks as a theme. They may choose cuckoo clocks, pendulum clocks, or some form which departs completely from a realistic image. In addition to sensing different rhythmic patterns, they may change dynamics by varying their use of space and force. Although improvisation may or may not be limited to one theme, it is directed toward capturing and refining the sensuous aspects of a particular problem.

The structure for improvisational experiences is open ended and lends itself to both individual and group participation. Whether the problem is suggested by a child or is set by the teacher, a child may function completely by himself. Those who choose to work together, however, must devote their efforts to the needs of the group as a whole. Here again exploration yields to improvisation. Although a child may initially explore his own movements according to his interpretation of the problem, he ultimately must adapt his needs to the interests of group expression. Because dance is nonverbal, the challenge is to communicate and relate kinesthetically to the movements of others.

For the teacher the value of such a structure is that it allows her to support and reinforce expressive qualities by pointing out innovative movements which may, at that moment, go unnoticed by a child. She must be able to accept a child's ideas, perceive an exciting movement, and make him consciously aware of it so that he can elaborate upon it if he so desires. In this way teachers can develop their own sensitivity in designing problems which continuously draw upon children's movement cues. By emphasizing a conceptual rather than a technical approach, they can elicit responses which lead to spontaneous, inventive solutions.

Concern as to whether movement is

spontaneous or imitative frequently arises among teachers. There is a tendency to accept rather standardized categories in education which may limit the perception of a child's behavior. The notion, for example, that a child "pretends" to be something rather than "being" it, in the sense of freshly experiencing it, conveys to children the idea that they are simulating rather than formulating movement. In the same vein, the idea that children are "imitating" needs to be reconsidered.

Dance as an art form is both an impressive and expressive experience. Although the act of dancing is expressive (that is, from the "inside out"), it draws upon impressions in the environment (from the "outside in"). Thus, spontaneity does not occur in a vacuum, but emerges from sensory data which provides the sources for expression of ideas or moods. But children do not passively receive sensory impressions; they deepen and clarify what they perceive by imitating or responding in some physical way to what they see, hear, touch, or feel. In order to be spontaneous, children must have a broad range of experiences in movement which call forth their imaginations and allow them to put together new combinations of ideas.

The relationship between interpretative and imitative movement is very subtle, yet is always subject to evaluation by a teacher. Because directly or indirectly, a teacher becomes a sponsor of values and an arbiter of attitudes, her own judgments as to what is imitative cannot help affecting children's perceptions of themselves. In most instances the quality of expression she elicits from children is in direct relation to the models and expectations that she sets. Inadvertently she may create an image of herself as a "model" by assuming that her role is to demonstrate movement in order to clarify it, a pattern immediately recognized by children as "follow me." In so doing, children respond to the expectation of being judged in terms of how accurately they can copy a movement. This is particularly diverting because an adult's size, shape, and use of movement elements are in no way comparable to those of a child. Perhaps a more serious implication is that when a teacher does it, it must be the correct way. There are times when a teacher's gestures are appropriate in guiding an observed movement, but the intent should be suggestive rather than prescriptive (that is, suggestive of ideas which help a child find forms of expression within his own body structure).

The differences between imitation and interpretation must be viewed in the light of our knowledge that a child's physical coordination, past experiences, and personality condition his responses. Whatever feelings are aroused as a result of the interaction of environment, teacher, and content, can only be expressed through the body as a result of a child's own perceptions. He may admire what another child is doing and want to try it. Some imitation is sometimes necessary for a child who feels initially self-conscious in moving out on the floor. He may begin by imitating another's movement and perhaps may even incorporate it into his own. But imitation of another's movement is never an exact duplication, any more than a child is capable of repeating his own movement when called up to perform it a second time. Some movements may be investigated consciously or may come about by an initial understanding of purpose; some will be found by seeming imitation; some will be "learned" or "taught." In any case, continuous encouragement by the teacher of momentary fragments of interesting movement will gradually turn children away from imitation and will help them appreciate their own efforts toward individual exploration.

No matter how the process unfolds, it is important to recognize that improvisation is an essentially individual, emotional response to a stimulating experience. Two children may respond almost the same and their movements may contain elements of imitation, but this is part of the process. Because a child can never duplicate a movement or impression exactly as he perceives it in nature, or as executed by someone else, he must search for his own forms. If a child has become more sensitive in his feelings and in his use of the body to interpret them, and if he is able to express ideas with a different insight or understanding than he had before, this is what may be expected in terms of developing interpretative responses. Each improvisation is an experience that is of value in and of itself and that, over an indeterminate period of time, forms the qualitative stepping stones in the creative dance process.

Just as explorations lead to improvisations, so may improvisations serve as preparations for *dance studies*. Although it is typically older children who have the interest and sustained drive to develop an idea into a more structured form, children at the primary levels may also be inspired by a topical theme or special celebration. Dance studies usually evolve from improvisations which have been repeated and refined as successful expressions of a particular problem or complex of problems. As children improvise, whether in response to an abstract concept, a specific movement, or a particular image, they find that certain movements appear that are satisfying to both their kinesthetic and their aesthetic sense. It is these movements which tend to be repeated and which, with subtle guidance from the teacher, become part of each child's unique movement vocabulary.

The concept of a vocabulary does not imply a stringing together of loosely connected movements, any more than a verbal vocabulary is composed of separate words that are mechanically put together. One motion does not make a rhythmic statement, just as one word does not make a sentence. To draw an analogy between these two types of language, basic locomotor and nonlocomotor movements make up the grammar of movement, improvisations are the syntax, and dance studies are presented metaphors. To speak of an individualized movement vocabulary means that each child takes the fundamentals of movement, combines them in varying dimensions of space, time, and force to produce his unique style. Style is not meant to imply a skillful device; it is the qualitative or sensuous

aspect of movement which emerges from the interrelationship of ideas, moods, or emotions and the manner in which they are given form by the body.

Although improvisations are built upon explorations of basic movement elements, dance studies are purposefully conceived and designed. Through conscious repetition, certain improvisational forms become elaborated and extended into fixed patterns which express a particular theme or themes. Unlike improvisation, which may begin and end at any point, dance studies usually have a beginning, middle, and end, so that there is a sense of development, elaboration, and closure. The process is one of inventing movements into structural dance forms which may be repeated.

Because we have come to depend so much upon the written word, it is important that teachers recognize that dance studies are neither stories that must accurately follow narrations in books nor dramatizations. Although there are dramatic aspects involved, dance is not storytelling. For example, a class may be studying the city as part of social studies, in terms of its transportation, traffic, streets, and buildings. Because the sights, sounds, and movements of the city pervade the sensibilities of contemporary children, they may draw directly upon these experiences, or they may select sensory images as a theme for a dance study. In either case, what is being created is not a representational statement of what actually exists in a city, but a metaphoric statement of abstracted qualities which symbolize forces or objects.

In seeking to capture the shapes in a city, for example, angles and corners are not depicted literally, but are projected through body shapes which give the illusion of buildings, street signs, and so on. The feeling of crowded and open spaces may be described by movements and countermovements in space, by tension and release of force, and by changes in beat and tempo. Children need not even locomote to express the chaos of traffic, but can create impressions of frenetic motion by the use of body parts in relation to each other.

Dance study has been defined as a presented metaphor in the sense that it is a connecting of diverse experiences by means of symbolic forms or images. In an art form the essence of the metaphor is that it seeks the common in the dissimilar, in this case, the impressions of a city through the idiom of dance. Thus, symbols are expressed through dance gesture which, as a language of its own, allows children to move beyond the common ways of experiencing their world.

2. *A conceptual framework for dance*

With an understanding and acceptance that dance is of vital importance in children's education, it becomes possible for a classroom teacher with willingness and sensibility to provide experiences in creative movement. Although rhythmic movement as it relates to dance is closest to a child in that his body is the medium of expression, it is the least practiced of any of the art forms. With little precedent for dance in elementary schooling, therefore, the question for teachers with no previous background becomes one of where to begin. For those already involved with dance, the question is one of stretching their horizons.

In either case, it seems simple to suggest that to begin is to move, but from what frame of reference? If learning is to be a coherent process, it must reside within a context, especially in the arts, where each encounter tends to be reduced to a fragmented activity. Just as there are central ideas in science and social studies, so there are basic concepts about movement which must be understood by both teachers and children. The difference, however, is that dance departs from conventional subject matter in that there is not one mass of material to be learned, one set of learnings does not necessarily lead to another, and evalua-

tions of what has been learned demand different criteria.

Perhaps a beginning lies in the recognition that the arts, and specifically dance, represent a way of *knowing* as well as a way of *feeling*. As a field of knowledge in its own right, dance contains a definition and description so that we may understand what it is, as well as what it is not, special characteristics which involve a unique experimental approach, and particular elements or media through which each child's expression is given form. The definition of children's dance and the nature of gesture as its distinguishing characteristic have been discussed in the previous section. To make dance come alive, however, we must turn to the immediate context in which it exists, and to the elements through which it takes shape as a living experience.

Movement comes into being within a framework of space–time–force which enters our lives on both a conceptual and perceptual level. Each plays a central role in determining ways in which a human being responds to his environment. Although they exist as physical properties of which we are almost unaware, and to which we respond almost routinely, in an art form they also exist as aesthetic qualities. As such, they function not as technical elements but as qualities used in expressing emotions and sensations, which are perceived uniquely by each individual.

Working within this conceptual framework allows teachers as well as children to become aware that although space–time–force exists in the external environment, these same elements are transformed in dance according to how and what a child wishes to express. Stated briefly, the body moves in and through *space*, which requires *time*; and since movement functions in relation to gravity, use of body weight or *force* is introduced. Put together in unique combinations, they become the means through which movement is explored through the full scope and potential of the body. As subjective, aesthetic elements, they take on meanings quite apart from the actual physical dimensions in objective reality.

If we contrast these two aspects of experience, we can examine the difference between the objective and the perceptual, or the "real" and the "feeling" world. In the physical world, *space* becomes known to a child through shapes, sizes, and relationships between objects. It involves ideas about his own body in space, objects, and spatial relationships within the environment to which he orients himself. On a perceptual level, an awareness of

space begins with the body and involves two conditions: (1) that the body is the center of reference, which determines the way a child uses space, and (2) that movement is focal in space perception. Thus, because movement is the essential ingredient in the exploration of space, the elements of space which a child uses will, in turn, affect the quality of his movement.

As he becomes increasingly aware of the dimensions of his body, he also becomes aware of the dimensions of other people and objects. For example, in response to the problem of creating the shape of a box with a partner, the space that is designed is not judged by metrical standards, but in terms of the way a child relates to another body shape in creating a new space. Similarly, a child's response to "How high can you be?" is not measured by a yardstick, but in relation to how and what elements he selects (level, direction, range) to extend his body in space. It is the difference between geometric space as defined by objects and the space which he defines by his body as he executes a movement or a series of movements. What is important is that teachers realize that a child's response to space as projected in dance form is not rational or logical as it must be in everyday living,

16

but is expressionist and kinesthetic. In other words, it is "felt" space.

Time in the physical world includes both clock and calendar intervals. It is initially experienced from the rhythms of the body through heartbeat, pulse, breath, which are cyclical. Whether children can "tell time" or not, time is sensed as units arranged in a sequence, which has continuity. Both clock and calendar time fit into a fixed pattern that is conventionally understood and accepted. But one "hour" presented in a movement is not equivalent to an hour of real time. A feeling of duration may be expressed as a sustained swing of the body or a circular movement of the arm, depending upon the type of imagery involved. Similarly, the time it takes for a child to go "from here to there" may be important only in relation to the rhythmic pattern he establishes, in terms of defining his own accented and unaccented beats. As with space, time is felt emotionally, in that the time a child uses for movement serves his own perception and is uniquely his. It is a created sense of duration which may be compressed or extended. To a child a unit of time may be great or small, long or short, past or present. Thus, each movement exploration represents, in part, a temporal order which a child imposes according to

his own needs, and exists entirely within a particular, direct experience.

Physical *force* involves weight, gravity, energies in motion, and relationships in space. In dance, force is a component of space–time and is experienced as the flow and control of energy. Because energy or force is the source of movement, it is also the basic ingredient in giving movement its aesthetic qualities. By varying the amount of energy expended, and by releasing energy in different ways, different qualities of movement are produced.

Force is sensed as tension which children feel kinesthetically in their own bodies. For example, it is one feeling to push against a real wall, it is a different sensation to push against a nonexistent wall, and still another to push against the resistance of another child's body. In the expression of a particular feeling tone, children sense that the amount of tension, stress, or force applied to a movement will significantly alter its time pattern, often its space, and always its meaning. In dance, the energy factor is one of the strongest means of communication, for it is responsible for variations and dynamics, that is, the texture and tone of movement.

Children's need to symbolize feelings and ideas through movement are given

I: Dance as knowing and feeling

The space–time–force used in movements are transmitted through this muscle sense, but the degree of kinesthetic sensitivity is dependent upon the emotions which stimulate the initial movement. Dalcroze, for example, who developed a system of body movement which he called "eurythmics," defined dance as the "art of expressing emotions by means of rhythmic bodily movements." [4] It was his belief, more than thirty years ago, that movements are capable of expressing all human emotions and that physical training directed toward artistic ends would make such unlimited expression possible.

In a strict sense, kinesthetic perception is the result of an awareness of sensory data (that is, visual, auditory, tactile); and the muscular system acts as an integrating center through which a child learns to orient himself in space–time. In a broader sense, a child's ability to move with fluency depends upon his feelings of "rightness" or "wrongness" in relation to how he can adjust and control his own body parts. The process is actually one of a combination of awareness and control,

both of which function interactively. If movement is to be of most value to a child, he must be able to express his unique way of feeling, moving, being; therefore, movement must always be "right" for him. Because kinesthetic perception is related to motor learning, it is essential that children become consciously aware of the feeling sensations of movement.[5] This points again to the idea that technique alone is not sufficient and that the search in dance is for the sensations and qualities of expression which accompany each movement pattern.

An aesthetic awareness of movement requires a kind of sensitivity that develops gradually from experiencing and feeling. Through the infinite uses of space–time–force, children come to realize that hands, feet, and head are capable of moving at different speeds and with different intensity, that the torso can show heavy and light movement, and that the whole body can speak for them as an expressive medium. Just as no two children talk in the same way, with the same inflection, intonation, or use of language, so no two

---

[4] Emile Jaques-Dalcroze, *Rhythm, Music, and Education*, trans. by H. P. Rubenstein (New York: G. P. Putnam's Sons, 1941), p. 232.

[5] Alma Hawkins, *Creating Through Dance* (Englewood Cliffs, N.J.: Prentice-Hall, Inc., 1964), p. 36.

children move alike. Although dance is an art form through which quality may be achieved equally well through group participation as by working alone, the success of a movement experience depends upon a child's unique ability to conceive of space–time–force in relation to his own body, and to control these elements imaginatively. In so doing he learns that he can impose an order upon his environment and that he can speak through emotional forms which have a larger scope than self-expression.

3. *A conceptual movement vocabulary*

In addition to the need for a conceptual framework there is the need for a conceptual vocabulary, because dance is a nondiscursive form of expression. Although we cannot "talk" dance, we can communicate concepts. If these concepts are to become integral to the dance experience, teachers need to develop a language that is flexible in permitting variability of expression yet precise enough that children understand the sources of their creative efforts. For teachers it provides the possibility of weaving the basic concepts of space–time–force into a comprehensible vocabulary for children. For children it offers a viable means of understanding how the elements with which they are directly involved take on subjective, aesthetic forms. The value of such a vocabulary is that it emanates from the elements of dance itself and helps to define those qualities that are usually left to the ephemeral.

There is a paradox in the sense that when children are in the act of moving, they are not concerned with conceptual forms, but with movement forms. At the same time, they need to understand the concepts from which their movements take shape. The vocabulary offered to children at the point of production, therefore, must be a functional, working vocabulary that is translated from verbal to movement terms. As formulated in the lessons here, it lends itself to both instruction and evaluation because it is inherent in the problems presented. It is a language that can be shared by teachers and children alike, because it is simple and direct and completely in keeping with the lexicon of dance. For teachers it is the difference in communicating meanings between "which way are you going?" and "what is your direction in space?" between "push as hard as you can" and "feel the tension or force in your arms."

Using language in eliciting responses to an art form requires a delicate balance for teachers; enough to make instructions clear and nonprescriptive but not so much that children become preoccupied with verbalization and lose the intent of the experience. Overemphasis on verbal preparation tends to reduce children's spontaneity and they are "talked out" before they even explore the possibilities of movement itself. It is for this reason that the vocabulary built into each lesson is designed to lead children immediately into the dance experience with directions that are clear and concise.

Teachers' verbal cues can be very helpful, however, with such comments as "we can't talk dance; your body will speak for you"; or when children tend to "explain" their movements where there is ambiguity, a comment such as "it's not important that we understand every movement; it's the over-all quality that speaks to us" places the focus where it properly belongs. Helping children to develop a language which appropriately describes the nature of a given experience also offers them a vehicle for self-evaluation and for constructive criticism of others. As children learn to identify the internal aspects of a problem in terms of its concepts and elements, there is less tendency to rely on judgments such as "I like it," or "I don't like the way he did it," which is enlightening neither to the observer nor to his peers.

Dance becomes an important experience when children begin to understand that just as they have a personalized way of speaking, so do they develop a unique way of moving. Because terms like space–time–force have subjective connotations in dance, the function of a conceptual vocabulary is that it stimulates movements which encourage exploration and does not impose specific forms to be followed by all children. Such a vocabulary provides a means of working with these elements singly and independently, to help children grasp the development of each one in greater depth. At the same time, however, a child soon comes to realize that the moment any one quality or element is changed, an entirely new movement comes into being. Although these elements are explored singly in all their dimensions, children begin to organize them into patterns which reflect their own needs and interests. In so doing, a child learns that there are many ways in which a movement can be executed.

Once a child recognizes that as an individual he moves in ways that are unique to him, he can appreciate his ability to develop his own movement vocabulary. When he becomes attuned to the notion that he can make his own statement through movement, there is less need to imitate movements of others which may not be coherent with his physical and emotional self. Exploring one's own repertoire gives children clues as to whether a movement is harmonious with his body structure and whether it best serves to express his emotions, moods, or ideas. Children tend to repeat the movements they enjoy, and an observant teacher can readily identify and help children become aware of the feeling qualities of their own movements. Thus, although we cannot reduce the lived experience of dance to verbal equivalents, we can help children give expression to both the knowing and feeling aspects of dance, which they can mould and synthesize into tangible, symbolic forms.

4. *Fundamentals of movement*

An awareness of space–time–force as the essential components of dance develops initially from explorations of movement fundamentals. Andrews[1] defines three categories which may appropriately be used here:

1. *Locomotor movements* which propel the body from one place to another *through* space, as in moving "from here to there," including walking, running, leaping, jumping, hopping, galloping, skipping, and sliding.
2. *Body movements* which project the body *in* space and emanate from a fixed base around the axis of the body from a sitting, standing, kneeling, or lying position, including bending, stretching, swinging, swaying, pushing, pulling, turning, and twisting.
3. *Combinations of movements* which may involve two or more locomotor movements (running and sliding), a series of body movements (pushing and pulling), or a combination of locomotor and body movements (running and swinging, walking, and stretching).

[1] Gladys Andrews, *Creative Rhythmic Movement for Children* (Englewood Cliffs, N.J.: Prentice-Hall, Inc., 1954), p. 38.

In dance those movements are characterized as fundamental which project the body in space using the feet as a fixed or moving base. Locomotor movements are most familiar and comfortable for children because they are most frequently used in everyday activities in covering space. Although we build on the "natural" movements of children, dance is a means by which such movements may be controlled and given new, expressive shapes.

Although the preceding examples are all fundamental movements, they vary in space and time, most distinctively in the way energy or force is expended. For example, in a walk, leap, or gallop the weight is transferred from one foot to another; in a jump or hop the weight is centered on both feet while the body is elevated. Most simple locomotor movements may be observed as part of children's spontaneous bodily activity. When the focus is on the qualities of the individual movements, however, confusion arises over changes in body weight, such as in the difference between a skip and a gallop, or a jump and a leap.

In order to help teachers visualize the characteristics of each locomotor movement, a brief description will be offered.

Walking low

It should be kept in mind that although these movements are executed primarily in the legs, the actual distribution of weight is controlled from the torso. Thus, if the muscles in the center of the body are allowed to "collapse" or if they are not engaged in the action, locomotor movements tend to become mechanical and lack buoyancy.

Locomotor movements

Walking carries the body through space by transferring the weight from one foot to another in a smooth, even rhythm; as the weight shifts, one foot is always in contact with the floor.

Running is walking at an increased tempo and with more force to impel the body through space; the weight is transferred alternately so that for a moment both feet leave the floor at the same time.

Leaping transfers the weight from one leg to the other which carries the body in an upward and forward direction; the feeling is of "pushing and reaching"; that is, the back leg pushes off the floor, the front leg reaches forward, and each foot lands *alternately*. A leap covers a greater distance and range in space than a run.

Leaping (a)

Leaping (b)

Leaping (c)

Jumping propels the body in space by pushing off the floor with the weight equally distributed in both legs; the body is suspended at the highest point and then submits to gravity by landing, with legs extended, on both feet, followed by bent knees from the force of the body.

Hopping carries the body upward in space, pushing off and landing on the same foot; the weight is centered over the hopping leg but is also sustained in the torso; the knee of the opposite leg may also be flexed to aid in elevating the body.

Galloping takes the body through space in a forward and backward rocking motion; the weight is carried on the forward foot on the longer or accented beat while the backward foot steps on the shorter beat; it is the simplest of the uneven rhythmic patterns because the feet do not change their relationship.

Leaping (d)

30

Jumping (a)

Jumping (b)

Jumping (c)

Jumping (d)

32

Skipping is a combination step–hop; the step gives impetus to the hop, which lifts the body upward in space; the higher the knees, the more buoyancy. It is similar to the gallop in that there is a transference of body weight, but it differs in that one foot always alternates with the other. This is the most difficult of uneven rhythmic patterns because of the alternation of feet.

Skipping

33

Sliding carries the body in a lateral position through space in a step-together motion; the weight may be equally distributed between the legs or additional force may be given to the accented step as in a sideward gallop. In a smooth, even rhythm there is a slight lift of the body as the feet come together. In an uneven rhythm there is increased elevation; the knees are always relaxed and both feet are in continuous contact with the floor.

Body movements

Body movements also derive from conventional activities in daily life such as bending, pushing, pulling. Instead of traveling through space, however, the body shapes the space by moving within it, in greater or lesser dimensions. Unlike locomotor movements which involve the whole body, these movements may be formed by the head, arms, legs and torso, alone or in combination. Movements radiate from the axis of the body, with the lower torso, legs, and feet acting as a fixed base. Because they require a greater awareness of how energy is released and

because they demand more control of body weight or balance, they are more difficult for children than locomotor movements. For purposes of simple description, they will be defined in relationships as follows:

1. *Bending* and *stretching*. Bending is a flexing or contracting movement in which two body parts are brought together inward toward the center of the body; the effect is to compress the body into a smaller shape of curves or angles. Stretching is a flow of energy in any part of the body which moves in a direction away from the center on a vertical, horizontal, or diagonal plane. They are not opposite movements, for one is the direct result of the other; that is, each time a part of the body bends, there is a stretch on the opposite side.

2. *Pushing* and *pulling*. Both pushing and pulling involve the extension or release of energy against a resistant force (real or imagined). Pushing is a movement outward, away from the center of the body and away from a fixed base. Pulling is a reversal of energy into the body moving toward a fixed base.

34

Bending and stretching (a)

Bending and stretching (b)

Jump, jump, twist (a)

3. *Swinging* and *swaying.* Swinging is a circular or arclike movement which shifts the weight up and down, side to side, or around; it is a feeling of "reaching and dropping," like a pendulum motion in which the impulse comes not only from the arms but from the torso. Both movements have a similar quality, but it is the nature of the impulse that makes the difference; that is, swinging is more gravitational and uses more energy in that it may be sudden and then down. Swaying is a rocking movement from side to side, or forward and backward, in a smooth, even tempo. It involves less energy than a swing, is more contained in the torso, and has a more limited range in space. There is less feeling of suspension than in the swing in that the impulse is of easy relaxation and recovery.

4. *Turning* and *twisting.* Turning is a revolving movement around the axis of the body and tends to have a cyclic pattern; if the body rotates on one level, a complete circle is formed; if the impulse carries the body on different levels or planes, a spiral or open circular pattern may result. Twisting is a rotation of the upper part of the body while the lower part remains stationary; although the weight is usually propelled from the torso, the arms can rotate from the shoulders, as

36

Jump, jump, twist (b)

Jump, jump, twist (c)
Jump, jump, twist (d)

Jump, jump, twist (e)

can the legs from the hips. The impulse
builds up a sequential rather than a simul-
taneous rotation, that is, a rippling action;
the amount of force affects the tempo
(fast or slow) and the quality of tension
(relaxed or intense).

Combinations of locomotor and body
movements will be explored in the lessons. Although each of the movements
described in this section is fundamental
to a child's developing movement vocabulary, they should in no way be regarded as
exercises. To do so would be to approach
movement purely as physical training and
to divest it of its dynamic, creative qualities. Mastery of one "step" does not guarantee the successful execution of another.
The problem in dance is not how well a
child performs a movement in isolation,
but how these movements relate qualitatively to each other as a total visual–
kinesthetic statement.

Opposite: Walking and stretching

5. The teacher as dance-educator

At the core of any meaningful dance program is the child as a creative being, the teacher who challenges his potential, and the content that she selects. The challenge is actually twofold. For the teacher it lies in designing dance experiences that are relevant to both the child and the content. For the child it lies in the nature of the exploration, wherein he becomes a creator, performer, and critic of his own work. One of the unknowns in education is whether we are developing any new capacities for creative efforts or whether a child's existing capacities are being allowed to flourish and deepen. Ultimately it rests with the teacher to initiate an environment that stimulates either condition.

Involvement in the creative process demands that the teacher consider herself not as one who "gives" dance to children, but as a dance-educator who can open new windows on the world for both the child and herself. A classroom teacher does not need the disciplined body of a dancer, but she needs to become actively involved in sensing her own feelings for movement. At the same time she must be sensitively aware that each child's movement speaks uniquely for him, and that this is a language which must be given expression.

It is unfortunate that dance in terms of the essential qualities described here has not received its due recognition as a necessary and integral part of elementary schooling. As a result, there are too few resources available for teachers who seek educational experience in this area. As more and more dance departments gain identity in colleges and universities, more classes in adult and children's dance will be offered through extension courses. It seems apparent that, just as teachers are encouraged to attend workshops in "new" math, social studies, and science, they should be given opportunities to turn their interests and talents to dance.

Introducing dance in the classroom as suggested in this book demands a search for an open approach which may bring certain traditional expectations into question. As with other arts, means and ends are inseparable, so that the process as well as the product must be given equal concern. Because it is the teacher who creates the climate, certain problems that are unique to dance bear thoughtful consideration.

For example, formal education has traditionally imposed the notion that learning takes place most effectively in silence. However, when the entire room becomes the center of activity and learn-

43

ing takes place through the body moving in space–time–force, we need to redefine the nature of the learning environment.

Experiences with children in any kind of movement activity reveal a commonality of response—the impulse of a child to burst forth in sounds. In the dance experience, where many children may be moving together, this may easily result in a din of confusion. The duration or intensity of those sounds is usually determined by the tolerance of the teacher, but beyond that, they must also reflect her understanding of how a particular group relates to a problem. That is, how long does it take them to formulate ideas, what is the learning style of these children, and how can they most effectively be guided into movement?

On the other hand, sounds which capture the function of certain types of imagery (trains, boats, planes, machines, animals) may add an enriching note. Just as children sharpen their kinesthetic sense through an awareness of how the body moves, so they may become conscious of how other senses are used to produce a unified expression. When viewed in relation to the problem itself, and not as an external source for discipline, teachers can make children aware of the critical

moment at which sounds begin to overpower their creative efforts.

A contributing factor in the balance between noise and silence is the premium placed on verbal responses in the school. In most situations children are encouraged to talk first and act later, but in dance the procedure is reversed. Shouting out ideas or attempting to describe a movement that has not been "felt" is inimical to the dance process. Discussion may or may not precede the presentation of a problem, but once children are out on the floor it is the body that speaks. Sounds, as words, must be impulses for the expression of the body rather than explanations of how the body is going to function. For the most part, after initial explorations, problem solving precludes vocal sounds, unless they are an inherent part of the problem. The excitement lies in making children aware that spoken language is not the only vehicle for thought and that they can find expression through the language of movement.

To this end much depends upon the quality of a teacher's voice, because it serves as an instrument in setting an emotional tone. Tone, in this sense, is an elusive quality that is easier to experience than to describe. It differs with each teacher in keeping with her personality, yet it is a common accompaniment which underscores the intensity and quality of each movement experience. Like any instrument, its interest for children lies in the variations in pitch, timbre, and texture; similarly, children lose interest in it when it becomes a monotone. Young children are quick to pick up cues not only from the spoken word, but from the voice quality behind it. For this reason teachers must be alert to the need for changes in dynamics (loud–soft, fast–slow, assertive–recessive) so that the spoken tone stimulates and supports the "tone" of the movement. If a teacher consciously listens to her own voice, she can make of it a sensitive instrument which communicates the quality as well as the intent of a dance experience (that is, the "how" as well as the "why").

Expectations as to an appropriate climate for dance actually reflect the larger issue of what constitutes order in the classroom. What has traditionally been described as disorder is really a question of whether everyone should do the same things or even finish at the same time (which gives the appearance of order). A child's use of time is a highly subjective aspect of the dance situation, as has

been noted, and each child's needs differ from one another. With this in mind, and within a given framework, a teacher must determine whether the confusion which occurs while everyone experiments in his own way produces a meaningful order in terms of inventive solutions.

On the one hand, there is the inevitable confusion of children searching through every sensory organ to relate their intentions to the control of their bodies. On the other hand, there are those children who, from time to time, do not actively participate but appear to be attentive. The question becomes one of trying to discern whether a child is comfortable as an observer and merely needs time to absorb what he sees or whether his self-consciousness prevents him from moving freely with his peers.

The extent to which children participate is always a concern of the teacher, but it is a concern for individuals, not simply for a show of numbers. The very nature of the creative process demands voluntary participation on the part of each child, because more is involved than responding to establishing patterns. It is implicit that each child feel the need to express himself and know that he will not be judged in terms of the group, but in

II: Creating an atmosphere for dance

relation to himself. Also, there is a great sense of pleasure when he can show his work to the group and receive their recognition for an interesting solution.

Familiarity with her own children is a distinct advantage for the classroom teacher, for what she observes in other areas of the program provides insights in this situation, as experiences in dance frequently reveal aspects of a child's personality not reflected elsewhere. Again, the response to individual differences calls for sensitive judgments. Children who do not easily participate must be given their own time, yet they need to be encouraged by teachers as well as children to feel that they belong and are involved, if only on a less active level. Unless a child poses a critical behavior problem, it is unlikely that he will remain detached from the group for long, for enthusiasm and creative energy are contagious. The crucial factor is not whether a child is functioning alone, but whether he has the individual freedom and opportunity to work alone or in pursuit of a shared experience.

There are many alternatives in any teaching situation which must always be weighed against the intrinsic elements of the material involved. Teachers have the option of directing learning in prescribed sequences, or of structuring problems that allow for the confusion of "constructive chaos" that is inherent in the way children grapple with their own solutions. Although the latter requires more time and more acute observation of children's efforts, their responses will unfold not according to a teacher's preconceptions, but in relation to their receptiveness and sensibility. Under these conditions a teacher is better able to judge her effectiveness in communicating and extending an emotional ambience suitable for dance. Thus, the alternatives chosen may release a teacher to become more perceptive and artistic in her own right, or they may keep her restrained, so that dance is merely something else to "give" to children instead of a pleasurable experience.

One traditional expectation that has left an impression on contemporary education is that dance is a feminine activity. As a result, many teachers tend to expect more participation from girls than from boys, since they appear initially more receptive. But just as teachers become aware that certain children participate more frequently than others, so must they become aware that complete exclusion is inappropriate.

Children vary in their response to a dance program. Some will demonstrate considerable inventiveness as soon as dance is made available; others will confront this activity with hesitation. As the program develops and becomes an accepted part of children's life at school, teachers will find that not only are children searching for individual means of expression, but they will be working effectively with others in solving movement problems. In the latter case, there should be little question of combining the sexes. When the focus is on the problem to be solved, boys and girls should freely choose each other or readily accept a child suggested by the teacher.

As teachers become more flexible in establishing grouping patterns to suit different kinds of explorations, children will become involved more diversely. If the participation of boys is an inherent expectation of each dance session, problems should be structured to ensure their involvement. This is particularly important in the light of perceptual–motor studies which have revealed that basically boys are more kinesthetically oriented than girls. It has thus frequently come to pass that as boys receive recognition for their efforts from teachers and peers, they become the dominant performers.

Inspiring a healthy working relationship between girls and boys is closely related to the expectation of how children should regard their bodies in dance. Here again children's attitudes reflect learned responses derived from cultural mores. In dance bodily contact is an inherent and necessary aspect of the total process. Just as children become informed by their own efforts that dance gestures are not imitations of real-life movements, so must they also become aware that touching has a connotation different from that in everyday behavior. A tactile sense reinforces the relationship of one's body to another and is experienced as an aspect of yielding or resisting force, or energy. Children must learn to respect their own bodies as the medium through which they can express feelings and emotions, not randomly or chaotically, as in flailing around on the floor or in pushing someone down, but through dance forms which require discipline and control.

With very young children bodily contact is less of a problem than it is with older children because they are still very physical in their responses. As children approach third grade, however, they tend to become self-conscious as to what they think are "acceptable" sex roles. Activities which require holding hands are an effective means of making contact (circle games or simple folk dances) and may introduce a more open feeling toward working in close proximity with others. For young children, holding hands offers reassurance of the presence of another child; for older children sequences can be developed so that holding or touching hands is accepted as part of the expressive content of a particular movement.

Dress becomes especially important in this regard. Although this is discussed in the following section, it merits brief attention here. Wearing long pants by both boys and girls not only allows the body greater freedom of movement, but mitigates certain stereotyped responses that are distracting and irrelevant. If dance is to become another mode of self-knowledge, children must feel comfortable about themselves and specifically must learn to appreciate their bodies as a form with its own power of expression.

Finally, teachers must deal with expectations in regard to their own role. It is important to reiterate that there must be a new vision of the teacher's role in the creative process. Teachers must not see themselves as "technicians" or "mediators," but as dance-educators who recognize that all creativity deals with potential, of children as well as their own. Because we are not concerned primarily with skills and techniques but with the subjective qualities of communication,

what is necessary is a willingness from both teacher and child to become engaged in the dance experience.

Teachers do not have to participate actively with the children at all times, but their presence must be felt in a mutual self-searching and free expression of emotions. Creative individual exploration depends upon close interaction between teacher and child, and between child and child. Because knowledge of oneself does not derive from facts in the dance situation, but from the expression of feelings about ideas and things in the environment, much of teaching is based on intuitive judgments. To value a fragment of a movement and see its possibilities for further development, a teacher must draw at least from her own feelings and at best from some knowledge of dance.

A teacher's role in making use of material which elicits creative responses is of enormous importance. From the initial act of presenting a dance problem, or drawing upon constructive, spontaneous behavior of the children, her presence should be felt as a supportive individual. It is conceivable that dance, like any art, incorporates its own discipline, because the relationship of the means to the end is so important. Within the same process, both means and end involve the total functioning of the child, so that his energy is a resource to be channeled rather than a distracting influence to be suppressed. Creative experiences have many stages of development. Because all normal children are capable of going part of the way, the role of the teacher is to encourage all children as far as possible.

Commitment to any art form involves a very personal teaching style, and although it varies among individuals, it must be rooted in artistic insights which stem from both the knowing and feeling aspects. Thus, a teacher's role is crucial, because by the nature of the teaching–learning experience, her attitudes and values toward dance, toward the body, and toward children's capacities will release or inhibit creative tendencies. When teachers realize that their own potential is a powerful element, dance can offer still another path through which they can work with children in new and exciting ways.

the physical space around them, and they can only learn this through movement. Directions such as *forward, backward, sideward,* and *diagonal* are identified in relation to the perimeters of the dance area, and children begin to sense this as part of their developing spatial awareness. Once a child "feels" these different orientations within his body, he is prepared to respond to more complicated problems, such as the difference between body position and direction (that is, moving in one direction with the body facing in another, such as walking backward in a diagonal direction or turning in a straight path through space).

Planning for *space* involves *time* literally to "push back the desks." [1] If children are engaged in activities away from the classroom before dance begins, a teacher can utilize that time to clear as large a space as possible, depending upon the structure of the room. The most unobstructed area is usually the center, which can be defined by placing tables or desks sideways along the walls, with chairs pushed underneath, so that the seats are unavailable for sitting. Whether the space

is at the front of the room or occupies the central area, it must be ample enough for children to move at least in small groups at a time.

Children returning to the classroom usually respond eagerly to the novelty of a changed environment, which by its very presence has built-in expectations: where to sit (on the floor, which guarantees against falling off chairs); how to sit (in a group or circle around the teacher, which makes for a more intimate relationship and more modulated voices); and where to put shoes and socks (under the chairs or in some easily identifiable place). Although such expectations need to be reinforced verbally until they become routine, the physical environment is immediately presented for the purpose at hand.

Even very young children also respond enthusiastically when they are directly involved in arranging their own setting. Teachers new to dance typically divide their energies between moving furniture alone and trying to control the group, amidst the inevitable confusion. But when children are prepared for change and are encouraged to help make it happen, they usually cooperate willingly. Ultimately, a teacher will find that time is

---

[1] Taken from Albert Cullum, *Push Back the Desks* (New York: Citation Press, 1967).

53

used more productively when children are invited to contribute so that an atmosphere of shared anticipation prevails.

Within the dance situation itself, concern for space and time is reflected through *pacing,* so that the minimum time is spent in moving objects and the maximum time is devoted to creative efforts. In this instance, time has both an external and internal dimension, one of how much to allow for each dance session and the other of how much is necessary for a given dance problem. In regard to the first, teachers should attempt to devote thirty to forty-five minutes at least twice a week, and preferably daily. As with any learning experience that is held only once a week, there is a time lapse which makes it difficult for children to carry over and develop ideas which were initially explored. Although muscles do have memory and children remember much of the dance material, weekly sessions make it necessary for a teacher to spend a considerable amount of time recapitulating what was done before.

The second dimension is closely related to a teacher's sensitivity in observing children. As the teacher becomes more comfortable with dance and more perceptive of its qualities she will recognize that each child's use of time, like his use of space, is unique and may be very different from that of others exploring the same problem. Awareness of the qualities of an experience derives from pursuing it in depth, rather than fragmenting it by intruding many unrelated activities. For this reason the lessons presented in this book are designed so that the number of sessions necessary for each one remains at the discretion of the teacher. Much depends on how sensitive the teacher becomes in helping children extend ideas into more fully developed movement patterns, and by the same token, on how quickly she responds to their nonverbal signs of exhausting a problem. The focus is always on the qualitative or expressive aspects of the experimentation, not on how many activities have been "covered" in one session.

Even at the primary levels, when children become absorbed they are frequently capable of working with one problem for as long as twenty minutes. Although it is generally true that older children can sustain interest for a longer period, there is no time schedule that can be established in advance. It is a teacher's intuitive feelings, gleaned from observing and working with a group she knows well, which act as her subjective time sense. In every situation balance of space and time is the key: enough space so that children may move freely and yet not so much that they become scattered and disoriented; enough time for children to explore and develop concepts, but not so much that ideas become scattered and lose focus.

Dance is essentially a group experience, and children are usually eager to share their explorations with their peers. But because of limitations of time, it is not always possible for all children to demonstrate their efforts within one session. Although for certain activities full group participation is appropriate and desirable, teachers will find that one of the most effective ways of allocating space and time is through *grouping*. As a general procedure it may prove fruitful to divide the class randomly in half (with equal numbers of boys and girls), given the understanding that each will alternate as participants and observers.

A small group working in a larger area may engage in freer exploration of a particular problem than they would in a constrained space. Even if they choose to call in others to elaborate upon an idea, they can utilize the space that would ordinarily be occupied by many more children. In addition to making it possible for more children to demonstrate their work, the idea of alternating roles reinforces the

idea that because dance is both a kinesthetic and visual form, observation is essential. Observers must be encouraged to watch attentively so that they become kinesthetically involved in the movements being created by other children. Watching others grapple with similar problems helps children sharpen their perceptions and opens alternatives that they may include in their own movement repertoires. Here again it rests with the teacher to achieve a balance in the pacing of groups who alternately observe and perform.

Working in smaller groups also allows children to become more observant of their own explorations and more sympathetic toward the efforts of others. As a result, discussions or interpretations of an observed movement may produce judgments which focus more on the inherent qualities of solutions than on subjective criticism of the children themselves. Children's interest is heightened when they are given to understand that grouping involves not only those who choose or are chosen to work together but those who are observers as well.

Whether children work alone or in couples, trios, or larger numbers, the degree to which a teacher actively participates depends upon what is happening at the moment. For very young children more physical contact may be initially desirable, but they may soon be able to "find their own place on the floor," which is, for example, a way of defining their own space. Older children, whose intentions frequently exceed their abilities, may require a "touch and go" type of contact. In all instances teachers should feel spontaneous enough to move freely around the floor so that they are in a position to observe and make comments about interesting explorations. Because a teacher implicitly sets the tone for judgments, her observations must point to the particular elements of a problem which a child takes on for himself and to his unique search for solutions. For example, a comment such as "What kind of movement is Johnny using with his shoulders?" is more enlightening than "Look what Johnny is doing." Such an approach makes it possible to minimize self-consciousness and to select and call to the attention of the class those individuals or groups whose responses demonstrate inventive and diverse solutions.

Finally, the physical environment must reflect a concern for children's *physical comfort*. Over the years the change from desks nailed to the floor to mobile tables and chairs indicates some understanding of children's inherent need for movement,

but educators have yet to recognize that what children wear may also affect what they can do. Because conventions regarding dress still prevail through elementary schooling, classroom teachers might consider as preparation for dance, clothes which permit children to move with ease. As a practical suggestion, girls as well as boys should wear pants (long or short, depending upon the weather), because this tends to de-emphasize clothes and to focus on the important issue, movement. For example, pants made of "stretch" fabrics are particularly appropriate, for they permit children to experience greater tactile receptivity to movement and greater awareness of their own body shapes. In cases where there is still resistance to casual clothing, each child might bring a bag with shorts or pants which are easily slipped on and which may be kept in the classroom throughout the year. As an additional factor, we know from observing children that their preferred place is the floor, and in this situation, it is especially fitting that they should feel comfortable and unconcerned about using it freely as a structural unit. Dance is the appropriate time and place to make friends with the floor, to use it as a source of strength and as a surface for the body.

Just as we do not put gloves on children

when they paint, so shoes and socks should come off. Through tactual contact children develop a sense of balance from gripping the floor with their feet and become sensitive to vibrations which they sense as rhythm. Most important, the feet are the base of the body's support for both locomotor and nonlocomotor movement.

As earmuffs deaden the sounds of music, so do shoes inhibit sensations of the many ways in which feet can articulate. Apart from encumbering movement, they make for unintentional accidents which result in both physical and psychological pain. There is little more in favor of gym shoes or sneakers. They too are an additional weight, and although rubber soles prevent slipping, they also impede children from developing a sense of balance that comes from strong, flexible feet. Because children's natural inclination is to go barefoot, the expectation of removing shoes and socks may provide still another element of excitement in preparing the scene for dance.

Thus, an environment provides the culture through which the arts may be nourished creatively. Although there is no certainty that creative expression can be taught, as a process it must be permitted, summoned, and recognized. We know from other kinds of educational experiences that although children have potential ability, they cannot create out of nothing, but there are things and relationships in the environment which can provide an impetus. In order to call forth the natural attributes of children and encourage them to work effectively, the teacher must set the stage. Because dance itself is a physical phenomenon, its expression and the environment in which it takes form are inseparable.

7. *Presentation of dance experiences*

Dance experiences are presented in terms of problem solving through the use of movement elements in situations which permit children to understand, imagine, explore, and create. The conceptual framework provides the context for these experiences in a way which does not prescribe solutions but which allows for innumerable movement possibilities within it. The lessons presented in the following section are designed to involve children in efforts to externalize their ideas and emotions by perceiving new relationships which they can manipulate and control through the use of the body. They are intended to depart from routine body mechanics in which each movement (or group of movements) is performed in isolation as a task leading toward a given goal. Rather, they are formulated with a view to giving teachers and children a sense of the fluidity and continuity of movement, so that each experience becomes part of the totality of the body's movement.

For this reason the problems include more than the mere presentation of materials; they are designed to elicit creative responses as the child reveals himself through the language of movement. Although the material of dance is movement itself, in this context it derives from the experiences, feelings, and ideas of children and takes its sources from stories, poems, songs, images, and other content in the curriculum. In the process of investigating the infinite uses of his body, a child begins to create movements new to himself and to the environmental setting which encourages such explorations. What we are seeking is a quality of experience which involves spontaneity and imagination from both teachers and children and which is based on content rather than specific techniques.

The need for skills in dance emerges from children's growing sensibilities and from their efforts to coordinate and control their bodies. The dance experiences presented here are intended to provide opportunities to use skills already learned (some of the basic locomotor movements, for example) or still being learned in ways which continuously challenge a child's level of ability. As both teachers and dance-educators, we are concerned with two interrelated facets of a child's development: (1) with the effects that creating have upon his general attitudes and behavior and (2) with what he learns and produces as a result of his engagement in the dance process.

On the one hand, the development and refinement of skills must be seen as part of the totality of a child's perceptions and responses; on the other, they must be understood as the means whereby he is able to increase the range and depth of his expressive movement. This does not imply, however, that the introduction of new materials or techniques must always await the expressed needs of the child. Frequently the excitement of new ideas for modes of expression stimulates him to explore new solutions and to deal with previously felt experiences in new ways. It is inherent in the creative dance process that only through actual experiences with movement can needs become clarified.

The creative impulse reveals itself most freely in a nonjudgmental atmosphere, that is, one in which the child is free to explore all the possibilities of a given problem. For the teacher this means an approach which encourages children to experiment, improvise, and even pursue unproductive avenues of exploration. Equally important is that a child be permitted to discover for himself those paths which prove unproductive in relation to what he is trying to express. In light of our concern for the total personality of the child, we find that such exploration leads to self-identification through a consciousness of his strengths and limitations

with a creative medium. As a child becomes aware that he has succeeded in part in making tangible what he wishes to express in movement, he may sense a broadening of his personality by virtue of receiving recognition for even partial success. This type of involvement also sustains children's beliefs in their own intuitive feelings, so that they are not looking to the teacher for "right" answers, but to themselves for the pleasures of finding alternatives. As both an objective and a procedure, a child's efforts and accomplishments must be measured against his own developing insights rather than against static or imposed views.

It is in examining the structure of the lessons themselves that we see how these generalizations regarding the dance process may be extended in practice. Because the focus of this approach to dance education is conceptual, the material is organized around the framework of Space–Time–Force. The designation of Part III as "Concepts and Explorations" is meant to inform the teacher at the outset that the basic concepts are the intrinsic sources from which learning experiences and understandings are developed. With this intent each of the four chapters begins with a description of the concept as it is experienced in dance and a definition of the specific movement elements through which it is transformed. This is one aspect of knowing that finds its counterpart in the knowledge of what the body is doing as a moving, creating force.

Because each teacher has her own style and no two groups of children are exactly alike, specific procedures of "how to do it" are not spelled out. Rather, each problem is defined so that the teacher is aware of both the context and selected elements to be explored within it. The intent is not to reduce the lessons to techniques that teachers and children must follow mechanically, but to ideas which lend themselves to adaptation and improvisation as each session unfolds.

At the same time, the structure of the lessons permit children to channel their energies so that their efforts are directed toward whatever avenues they have chosen to pursue. Problems are presented in open-ended form so that children are constantly making decisions, not always consciously or cerebrally, but in the very selection of movements. This approach is in deliberate contrast with one of "everybody do what you want to do (to the music or the drum)," which sets no boundaries to children's investigations

and offers them no way to relate the conceptual idea with the expressive "doing."

There are no specific directions in relation to grouping other than what is implicit in the instructions to the children. Whether children work alone or with others depends largely upon the content of each lesson. Although certain general explorations lend themselves to full group participation, only a few children can demonstrate their efforts at one time. In some cases instructions include the number of children who should work together, but for the most part, it is left to the discretion of the teacher to assess the best working relationships of her particular group.

In each session it rests with the teacher to determine what is important and where the emphasis should be placed. If, for example, she feels that the children should become more aware of spatial orientation, she may involve two groups of children moving together to help them become conscious of ways in which they can relate to others as dancers or as objects in the environment. If the need is to work together rhythmically, she may select a problem in which partners respond to each other's pattern in a similar or counterpoint movement. To understand how the extension of force affects another body, children may be instructed to work in couples or trios to experience the "push–pull" or tension of another's movement. It is important that teachers establish the number of children who will participate initially. As the process takes shape, new solutions frequently give rise to new problems, which demands fluidity in the types of grouping that appear to be necessary.

Second, the statements of the problems are the major headings intended for teachers, whereas instructional cues in the form of directions, suggestions, and questions are worded briefly and concisely for use with children of all ages. In general, the language of the problems is designed so that children become immediately aware that there is a verbal as well as a movement vocabulary. Gradually, the naming of movements and qualities of feeling reinforces the knowledge that comes from their developing kinesthetic sense. For example, children are helped to discriminate between a skip, slide, and gallop if they name each movement as they execute it. The same applies to sensing the differences when walks change to runs and become leaps. Further, in a rhythmic experience where each child selects a movement which corresponds to the syllables of his name, a hypothetical Jon-a-than Pe-ter Bach-rach may say;

"run-run-run, leap-leap, jump-jump,"

so that the naming while doing reinforces a consciousness of his own rhythmic pattern.

On an objective level, children should become familiar with the terminology of movement so that they can express what they are experiencing with an economy of words. An appropriate movement vocabulary can be understood by children beginning in kindergarten if it is used substantively, for there is a language for problem solving in dance. For example, words such as *direction, level,* and *path* help children describe where they are in space; *beat, accent, rhythmic pattern* help them clarify their individualized sense of time; *percussive, sustained, swinging* movements help to explain the different ways in which they exert and control energy. Just as the language of mathematics does not elucidate in terms of poetry, so the language of dance is not conveyed through conventional speech; instead it is articulated in terms of its own images.

On an affective level, verbal expression becomes more difficult, for there is not always a relationship between what a child is feeling within himself and what he is able to communicate to others. It is the equation between communion with self and communication with others, as discussed in the first chapter. It is for this reason that children cannot always "explain" what they are doing, but may be able to express a feeling quality that is interpreted by others.

Because the forms of dance are non-discursive, it becomes even more important that there is a commonly understood basis for verbal communication between child and child, and between child and teacher. Even from the standpoint of efficiency, the use of a meaningful movement vocabulary reduces the amount of "talk" and explanation from both teachers and children. One word or combination of words may provide a significant cue so that there is little need to rely on protracted spoken instructions and children can turn their efforts immediately to the forms of dance. Thus, a child, even a very young one, while becoming aware of the myriad movements of which his body is capable, learns ways of naming, ways of designating qualities, and even ways of describing his feelings in dance terms.

Third, it will be noted that solutions are described in greater or lesser detail for most of the problems presented here. The intent is not to impose a prescriptive view of what children *should* or will necessarily do, but a description of movement possibilities which inform teachers of what children *can* do. All of the notations are transcriptions of observed responses of children from many different environments and classrooms and are intended to serve a dual purpose: to acquaint teachers with the diversity and variability of children's movements and to formulate a vocabulary which emanates directly from the dance experience itself. It may prove interesting and worthwhile for teachers to write brief observations of their own children's work throughout the year so that, in addition to establishing continuity, they are better able to think and speak in the language of movement.

III

Concepts and explorations of space–time–force

8. *Concept: space*

Although a child himself is three dimensional, in that his movements not only have length and breadth but depth and thickness, he still needs to discover how to use space. When we speak metaphorically of a line that the body makes in space, we are actually referring to a volume which fills or displaces that space. In working with children it soon becomes evident that any definition is meaningless unless it becomes functional for them. Through investigation of the elements of space, children come to realize that in order to cope with it, it must be occupied, contained, and defined.

A child needs to be made aware, for example, that as soon as he takes a place on the floor, standing or sitting, he defines that space by his very presence. That is, the area in which he exists becomes occupied. Even as he stands immobile he designs space, for we can see around him, follow the plastic lines of his body, and know that he has dimension. When he simply extends an arm or swings around the axis of his own body, he defines both his immediate (inside) body space and the outer (outside) space around him. If he engages in any type of locomotor movement, he is designing the space between himself as a body in motion and the walls or perimeter of the dance area.

Beyond this, it is the space between the child and other children or objects that has yet to be defined.

Because space is the most important single aspect of perception, establishing a relationship to the surrounding space has implications for a child's behavior in general. In this context it is also significant to recall that movement is the essential ingredient of space perception. This means that the body is the relative point of a child's spatial orientation toward the world and, at the same time, becomes one object among many objects in a contained space. In everyday behavior it is through extending the body's spatiality into external space that a child relates to and communicates with his environment.

In dance, perception of space is twofold: it is seen in relation to the body and in relation to the surrounding space. In order to understand and use space expressively, explorations should allow children to organize space in relation to themselves and to find modes of adjusting spatially to objects and other individuals. In very simple terms, children can be made aware of the space that lies within their own bodies through observing their own movements, such as rocking, twirling, or turning over. Similarly, they can perceive themselves in relation to the surrounding space by being in a constrained area with other children while attempting not to touch anyone or, conversely, by perceiving how the body moves in relation to things in external space by moving in and around other children or objects in an open area.

Whether children work alone or together, they must be conscious of one another, not intellectually but kinesthetically, in the sense of "knowing" it through the body. Depending upon the nature of the problem, a child should be able to determine whether others who are moving are simply part of his environment in the same way as objects, or whether his movement should relate to theirs. This holds whether a child works with others in small groups or whether he is working individually amidst the entire group. An awareness of who is around and what they are doing helps a child better understand spatial relationships and enhances his own sensibility.

The illusion of volume or direction in space is created by explorations of the basic elements, which are defined as *direction, level, range,* and *focus*.

Direction is the line of motion made by the body moving *through* space (for example, forward, backward, sideward, diagonal; turning is not a separate direc-

tion but is a combination of forward, sideward, and backward movements). In daily behavior children are continually called upon to respond to such directions as *forward, backward, sideward, and around*. In dance they have yet to discover how these directions function in relation to the position of their own bodies as well as to the surrounding space.

Stated simply, directions move up and down, in and out from the center of the body as the point of reference. Because of the structure of the body, the greatest ease of movement is in a frontal position, and therefore, in a forward direction. As both sides of the body are identical (handedness not withstanding), lateral space is more difficult to perceive (that is, moving from the side or discriminating between left and right). There is frequently confusion between taking a lateral body position and moving in a diagonal direction. In the former, all parts of the body must express the same diagonal feeling. In the latter, one may take any body position as long as the space is divided diagonally. Understanding lateral space is a developmental phenomenon and must be learned through consciously guided experiences. For this reason, a teacher must be aware of her position vis-à-vis the children when giving instructions which require a left–right orientation. For example, asking children to follow a lifting movement of the right leg while facing them is disorienting, for their inclination would be to respond with the same side of the body, which would be the left leg. Although it may not be necessary specifically to define *left* and *right* in the early years, exploring laterality is an important aspect of direction because it significantly affects the way a child organizes his space.

A movement through space is defined when all parts of the body follow the same directional line. A movement is *forward* when the front of the body is leading (for example, head, forehead, chest, nose, stomach, knees, or feet); it is *backward* when the weight is from the back of the body (for example, a backward tilt of the head, a rounded back, an extended buttocks, or a backward thrust of the legs); it is *sideward* when the impulse for movement comes from the side of the body (for example, the side of the head, shoulder, extended elbow, or hip). It is always a surprise to children to discover that turning is not a separate direction, but is a combination of the three which can be experienced by rotating the body slowly, taking one step in each direction. In so doing, they become aware that the

position or plane of the body remains frontal even though directions change, and that a turn may be executed in any spatial direction. Focusing on the direction of the body in space also increases a child's ability to identify the planes of the body (front, back, side) and to become acquainted with still another facet of how the body functions in both locomotor and nonlocomotor movement.

In order to clarify the difference between the use of internal and external space, a teacher's choice of language must be explicit. In children's terms, directions may be expressed as moving "from here to there," but the framework must be defined. Moving backward, for example, does not imply moving from the back to the front of the room, just as moving sideways does not necessarily mean going from one side to another. With experience children develop a sense of spatial orientation as they discover that they can slide in circles as well as sideways, skip backward toward whatever is designated as front, and experiment with combinations of movements in various directional patterns.

As well as moving *through* space, the body also moves *in* space on *levels*, which is sensed as a transfer of body weight from the center of gravity. Because each child has a unique body structure, the exact center varies with each individual. In any case, levels are expressed in relation to the body in terms of three dimensions. (1) *High* begins when the center of the body is shifted above its normal position. Because children typically respond to *high* by simply raising their hands over their heads, it may be relevant to clarify that for this use of space there must be enough tension in the body that the heels leave the floor, as in tiptoe, jumping, and leaping. Extending the arms may represent a stretch but there is no shift in body weight. (2) *Middle* exists when the trunk is in an aligned or upright position—as in walking, running, or turning—or when the upper torso is bent or extended at the waist in a forward stretch of the back, or in a lateral stretch of the arms. (3) *Low* is below the center of gravity in whatever direction is taken, as in walking with flexed knees, rolling, or any collapsing movement.

These spatial elements expressed through direction and level also reinforce learnings in other areas. Abstractions such as "how high is high," "how low is low," "how far is far" can be translated into concrete experiences which children can investigate in relation to their own size, shape, and organization of energy. No-

tions of *over*, *under*, *around*, and *through* take tangible forms through experiences such as moving through a body shape created by another child, around and over an object, or under one of his own body parts.

Moving in any direction produces *floor patterns*, which are designs made by the feet as they travel in various paths through space. Generally, such patterns are either straight or curvilinear and should be considered as part of the total design of the body. Children can be made aware that their feet as well as their bodies create "pictures" in space. Moving in combinations of straight lines, for example, may form squares, rectangles, triangles, or zigzags. Curved lines result from any variation of a circle or semicircle, such as moving *through* space in an arc or figure 8 or moving *in* space in a spiral or corkscrew design. Exploring different directions and patterns reveals that the body can cope with space in ways other than frontally and that the direction of a movement may impel the feet to form patterns which give the body more spatial freedom. In addition, floor patterns are frequently the rudimentary steps of folk dance and may help children become more receptive to this aspect of dance. It is conceivable that as children become

70

more inventive in their own designs, they find it easier to learn the structured patterns of square and folk dance.

Although a directional movement may be expressed as a line, it also has a size and shape. The shape of a movement may be curved or straight, depending on the nature of the line it creates. The size is defined as *range*, which is the amount of space the body occupies as it moves (for example, large–small, narrow–wide). Range applies not only to the space filled by the total body in motion, but also to the distance covered by the movement of a particular body part. Because the whole quality of a movement can be changed by the use of more or less space, children can explore range by deliberately varying the size of a movement in a given problem. By making it "big" or "little," expansive or restricted, they become informed through their muscles that this element functions as an expressive ingredient of movement. It should be borne in mind, however, that although we are dealing with an element of space, no concept exists in isolation. Therefore, changes in the range of a movement inevitably involve variations in time and force.

Moving through space in a controlled way ultimately requires *focus*, which is the most difficult of the spatial elements

for young children to learn. By definition it is the directional intent of an individual as he moves through space. In a sense, we are asking children to respond to a "see and move" relationship, either as separate actions or as actions occurring simultaneously. In one instance he may fix his eyes on a chosen point (perhaps on the opposite wall) and move toward it; in the other he may choose a spot on which to focus while moving. In either case the purpose is to help the body achieve direction so that the unity and balance of the body is maintained.

Focus is not an element that should be emphasized mechanically but it may be called to children's attention when a need emerges within an experience. In any type of locomotor movement, for example, a child will find that looking down at the floor or glancing randomly around the room restrains the body from moving freely and limits its spatiality. Turning, whether fast or slow, frequently makes children dizzy, because the movements are unfocused and uncontrolled. But a simple experience, such as walking backward or moving in large circular patterns, may also result in falling down or in some disorientation. It is at these moments, when needs for focus are observed, that teachers may encourage children to

71

"find a point on the wall with your eyes," or "look straight ahead." Although the word itself may be unfamiliar, the effect of its action will lead to an understanding that focus sustains the directional impact of a movement. Thus, the purpose of focus is to stabilize the body's movement in space.

As has been discussed, the body is three dimensional and has volume, and whether it is in a state of stillness or a form in the making, it creates its own *shape*. *Body shape* does not relate solely to the concept of space, for it draws upon all elements. However, we may consider that dance, as a visual–kinesthetic image, "shapes space," and the body is the medium through which this occurs. Body shape is not determined by a child's natural structural features, such as his height, width, or breadth, but refers to the shape that the body makes in space in forming expressive movements. Again, with the body as the center of reference children must become aware of two aspects of spatial orientation—the inside space, which is shaped by the way a child uses different parts of the body in relation to the torso (circular, angular, linear), and the external shape (around, above, below), which is occupied by the shape made by the total body.

In the process of exploration children come to realize that they can create many different qualities and types of shapes (for example, round, flat, heavy, filled, empty), that body parts in various positions make particular shapes, and that the actual shapes of their bodies are not necessarily the shape they are attempting to describe in dance terms. For example, triangles, circles, rectangles, and squares are shapes that children observe around them in the environment and learn about through different modes of investigation. Although it is not possible or even desirable to translate a geometric form literally in movement, children can sense angles, corners, or circles kinesthetically in their muscles. Beyond this they can create interesting abstract shapes which utilize both internal and external space by working out spatial relationships with others, either in harmony or in opposition to another body shape.

This aspect of space leads children further into an appreciation of their bodies as a medium of creative movement rather than simply an instrument of functional action. They learn that dance is not the shaping of the body for movement (for example, bending to pick something up) but that it is using the body to shape movement expressively.

The exploration of space to enhance the expressiveness of movement is made known to children as they experience changes in direction, level, range, and focus. Each of these may be explored as separate problems, for each has a different kinesthetic effect upon the body. At the same time, the very nature of the unity of movement is such that all of these elements function together and that each may lend a different and more developed quality to a dance experience.

Explorations in Direction

Problem I: To explore the use of different body parts as the impulse for direction *through* space.

A. *How do we get from "here to there" using different parts of the body? (The space from "here to there" must be initially defined for the children in relation to the dance area.)*

 1. When you walked into the room today, what parts of your body were leading you? (Children's responses: feet, toes, stomach, muscles.)
 2. You do not always have to walk with your feet leading you. For example, how would you get from "here to there" with your "behind" leading you?

    SOLUTION
    Crouching with knees flexed, buttocks extended backward, torso bent forward at middle level, arms loose at sides or extended and walking in backward direction.

 3. Let different parts of you take you on a walk through space; move freely around the room following in your own direction.

    SOLUTIONS
    Stomach: Back arched, abdomen forward, knees flexed, arms hanging down, head back with neck flexed; or back arched and abdomen extended, walking on hands and feet in crab fashion in forward direction.

    Big toe: Body erect; one foot extended, with weight on forward toe; back foot sliding; slow, galloping motion in forward direction.

    Knees: Both knees flexed, body in crouched position, knees, open and slightly turned out; lunging in forward direction.

    Elbow: One elbow flexed, with lower arm parallel to the floor; body in lateral position; moving sideways with feet sliding or cross stepping.

    Back: Back arched, head extended back, upper torso inclined backward, arms hanging at sides; walking in backward direction.

    Top of head: Head bent forward, body flexed at waist, arms hanging loosely at sides; walking in forward direction.

ADDITIONAL ELEMENTS   *Children become aware of the need for transference of body weight as different parts of the body are used.*

Problem II: To sense how qualities of force expended in different body parts give added impetus to direction.

A. *Feel that there is a string attached to some part of your body and let that part pull you through space.*

1. Let your forehead lead you; your nose; your chin (forward locomotion).

SOLUTIONS
Walking in straight line with forehead, nose, chin extended in front of body is controlled by forward thrust of the neck and flexion in the back of the neck. Weight is centered over the toes to the point where the pull of gravity increases the tempo of the steps. (Complete resistance to gravity will pull body to the floor.)

2. Move with your ear leading you; your elbow; your shoulder (sideward locomotion).

SOLUTIONS
Ear: Walking sideward in a straight line with straight or flexed neck with a lateral incline of the body in the direction of the line of movement; walking erect in sideward direction with neck flexed to extend ear. Foot pattern crosses over in front or back (similar to a folk dance step) in diagonal or circular path.

Elbow: Elbow flexed and lifted to shoulder level with body moving diagonally; line of direction is suggested by the elbow (awareness that wider steps contribute to the body locomoting sideways in space).

3. Walk where your heels take you; now let your back lead you; shift the weight to your back (backward locomotion).

SOLUTIONS
Heels: Forward or backward walk with feet so flexed that toes stretch off the floor; weight is centered in torso to maintain balance. (Force of gravity causes increase in tempo; if backward tilt of body yields to gravity, it may fall.)

Back: Both knees flexed in forward position, wide stride by back leg carries body in backward direction in an uneven, rhythmic walk.

B. *Now let's divide into three groups; while one group moves at a time the others will watch, then take turns.*

    1. This time feel the difference between *pushing* that part with your body and letting it *pull* you in the direction in which it is facing.

SOLUTIONS
Elaborations develop from the previous problems (that is, in "pushing," the weight remains in the torso and can push the body in any direction, regardless of the position of a particular part); "pulling" consciously shifts the weight to that part which determines the line of the body and the direction it takes in space.

Problem III: To establish a direction by coordinating the moving body with a fixed point in space.

A. *Just as we can walk with different parts of our bodies, so can we "point" to directions without using our fingers.*

    1. Look around the room; find three places to which you are going to move, each on a different level.
    2. Everyone take space on the floor; point to the first spot with some part of your body and keep moving in that direction until you touch it with your "pointing" part.
    3. From where you are point to the second spot with a different part of your body and approach it with a new part leading you.
    4. Now change the part of your body that will take you to the third spot.
    (If there are too many children for the space, a few may move at a time, beginning from different places; in the final exploration, children may be divided into small groups who are moving in the same direction, although with different body parts.)

SOLUTIONS
The type of locomotion and the direction in space depends upon which part of the body is "pointing." (That is, if a child points to a middle level and leads with his elbow, he may hop, slide, or take cross steps; if the level is low and his toe or foot is leading, he may

slide on his side, pushing with his hands, or, from a sitting position, he may propel himself by his hands so that the "pointing" foot remains forward.) A high level, depending on what part of the body touches it, may be reached by any of the forward locomotor movements, resolving in a stretch, jump, or leap.

ADDITIONAL ELEMENTS Focus, *which is explored in another problem, as well as* levels *in space.*

B. *Different parts of your body took you in different directions* through *space, and on different levels* in *space.*

   1. How many different ways did you use your body to get to your three spots?
   2. What kinds of movements took you through space?
   3. What directions did you go in?
   4. Let's watch a few people at a time and notice how the *lines of their bodies* change as they move in different directions, and what *shapes* their bodies make as they point with different parts.

Problem IV: To explore the relationship between body plane and spatial direction.

A. *Even when you are sitting perfectly still your body is a shape, just like any object in the room, and each side of you can use its own space differently.*

   1. The way your body is shaped helps you move in many different ways; your body may face one way, but you can still move in a different direction.
   2. You know that when rabbits hop forward they face frontward, but when frogs hop backward, they still face frontward.
   3. Let's explore to see whether being frontward and moving forward is the same thing.
   4. Take two steps forward, turn two steps to the side, turn two steps backward, two steps to the other side, two steps forward.
   5. In what direction did you move? Each time you changed direction, how was your body facing?

   SOLUTIONS
   Children are aware that they are *turning*; although they are changing directions, they are facing forward at all times (body

plane remains frontal); turning is a combination of all directions (frontward, sideward, backward) and may be executed in any spatial direction.

B. *Machines that work for us also move in different directions, and change their positions. Can you think of some? (Children's responses: steam shovel, snow plow.)*

  1. Find a place on the floor. How does a steam shovel work?
  2. Does it move in one direction?
  3. Does it always face the same way?

SOLUTIONS
Steam shovel swings around, moves forward, goes down to scoop up dirt, comes up with load of dirt, backs up; uses both locomotor and body movements.

ADDITIONAL ELEMENTS *Awareness of immediate* space *around body and external space involved in locomotor movement; use of* force *as impulse for directions of body parts; changes in* range *and* level*; rhythmic pattern* of *movements.*

Problem V: To become aware of new coordinations of body parts in locomotor movements.

A. *How many ways can you get from here to there without using your feet?*

  1. What parts of your body did you use to get across the floor? (Children may move across the floor three or four at a time, depending on the amount of space.)

  SOLUTIONS
    a. With weight centered on hands and shoulders, pulling across floor on stomach with both feet raised.
    b. With arms spread wide apart and weight centered in upper torso, pulling along on one knee, with back leg extended in air.
    c. Rolling over and over, with head and feet held away from floor.
    d. Crouching in forward position on knees, with feet flexed away from floor, arms close to body, knees walking with small steps.
    e. From a sitting position, propelling body backward and around by the arms.

f. Lying on back with both knees bent to chin, with hands pushing body in rocking motion along floor.

g. Attempts to elevate both legs and walk on hands prove unsucessful.

UNDERSTANDINGS FOR TEACHERS—PROBLEMS I–IV

How does a child move when an elbow or shoulder leads him in a sideward direction in space (as contrasted with conventional modes of locomotion)?

What do his feet do? How do his arms help him move?

How does he feel the different parts of his body "push" or "pull" him? What is the difference in the qualities of force (energy)? What happens to his sense of balance as he uses various body parts?

What shapes do his body make when his head, back, or knee lead him?

UNDERSTANDINGS FOR TEACHERS—PROBLEM V

What do children sense in the coordination of body parts? Can they relate their kinesthetic experiences to a movement vocabulary of such action words as "walking on my hands, rocking on my back, turning in circles on my behind, rolling on my side; pulling with my hands, pushing with my knees?"

Are children aware of the different types of locomotor movement they used?

How do they sense the need for redistribution of body weight in coordinating new body parts?

Explorations in Levels

Problem I: To understand levels as the direction of the body *in* space, described as "high, medium, or low" in relation to the center of the body.

A. *When we move from here to there, we are moving in different directions through space, but we can also move on different levels in space.*

B. *Let's explore levels of space on your own body. Where are they in relation to the space around you?*

1. Stand perfectly still with your feet together and your head and body in a straight line. Where is the middle level on your body? Where is it in space? Move out into space with any kind of movement but keep your body on a middle level.

   SOLUTIONS
   Walking forward with head and shoulders bent over waist, arms hanging at sides; walking forward with legs in wide stride, flat back stretched forward from waist, arms extended laterally; bending forward, with back curved and head and arms arched around upper torso.

   a. The middle level is not just in the center of your stomach; it is the whole area between your shoulders and your hips. Can you move on a middle level in space by raising, lowering, or extending parts of your body in different ways?

   SOLUTIONS
   Crouching in half-way position, with knees flexed, walking forward; bending the torso, with head almost to floor, back arched, arms swinging loosely; using arms freely, for balance and body shape.

   b. Put your weight on one knee and try all the possible ways of moving on a middle level. Now place your weight on both knees and see how many ways you can move in space.

2. Where is "high" on your body? Where is "high" in space? What direction are you moving in on this level?

   SOLUTIONS
   Standing erect, with arms raised; standing on tiptoes, with

arms stretched over head; jumping with both feet and with arms at sides; jumping on one foot, with opposite arm raised.

a. High is not just from the top of your shoulders to your raised finger tips; it starts from the moment that you lift the center of your body higher than usual.

b. How high is high? How high can you walk without actually leaving the floor? How high can you go if you

I.B.2

I.B.2b

I.B.2b

I.B.2b

leave the floor? Can you reach for more space? What parts can help you reach higher?

SOLUTIONS
Jumping with greater flexion in knees; pushing off the floor from a crouching position; jumping with feet brought up to buttocks; full body stretch with heel off floor, arms fully stretched.

3. Where is "low" on your body? How low is low in space?

SOLUTIONS
Initially, most responses are collapsing movements ending on the floor.

a. Can you find different low levels in space before you reach the floor? Your muscles will help you balance when you lower the center of your body.

b. How low can you go if you keep your feet on the floor? How much space can you use with your whole body on the floor? How little space can you use?

SOLUTIONS

Balancing on toes in crouching position, with head tucked in and arms encircling knees; crouching, with knees flexed and torso erect, arms at sides; curling up on side of body, knees touching chin, arms around knees; body curving forward, with buttocks off floor, weight on knees, arms forward in wide position, head on floor between arms; lying on back, arms and legs in diagonal position; lying on back, knees drawn up to chin, arms pressing legs to body, head bent forward on knees.

c. Now from some of these positions can you move *through* space on a low level?

SOLUTIONS

Walking on flexed knees, walking with knees flexed, rolling, sliding on stomach, pushing on back.

Problem II: To explore levels in space with locomotor and body movements using different sources of imagery.

A. *Think of all the different levels we move on when we work and play.*

I.B.3

1. Imagine that you are going to paint the walls of your very own room. Decide where these four walls will be and stay within that space.
   a. Pick up the bucket of paint without bending your knees; stir the paint with a big stick; and put it down slowly.
   b. Take a brush in one hand; paint the walls from top to bottom, from bottom to top, and from side to side; take long, even strokes and feel the weight of the brush as it moves in space.
   c. Now paint the ceiling; stretch to reach it. What happens to your body when you paint in that position? What parts of you are supporting your weight?

   SOLUTIONS
   Moving on all three levels in space and in different directions (up–down, sideways, circular); using various locomotor movements to get from wall to wall; using body movements such as bending and stretching (low to high); lateral swings or stretches (middle level); bending and stretching back and forth (high level).

   d. On what levels in space are you working? In what directions are you painting? What parts of your body are you using in addition to your arms?

   ADDITIONAL ELEMENTS   *Use of force in sustained movements redistributes body weight as directions change; creating a shape in space.*

2. What do you do with toys and blocks when you are finished playing with them? Put them away? Where? Yes, shelves are good places.
   a. Because there are no "real" toys lying around here, imagine that you are going to find a place and put your toys on the lowest, middle, or highest shelf.
   b. Remember, toys and blocks have different shapes, different sizes, and they do not all weigh the same. Your movements should show whether you are picking up something light, heavy, big, small, round, or square and on what shelf you are putting them.
   [If there are too many children for each to have his own place, two or three "shelves" (spaces) may be designated and children can move toward them singly or in small groups.]
3. Let's watch a few people at a time and see if their bodies

tell us what kinds of toys they are carrying and at what level
they are placing them.

SOLUTIONS
Levels may be reached by kneeling, bending, stretching; picking up toys of different sizes and shapes may involve bending, twisting, turning, lifting; very "heavy" toys may be moved by pulling or pushing.

B. *An elevator takes you up and down in space but may stop on many levels between high–medium–low.*

   1. You can be an elevator alone, with a partner, or with a group; if you work with someone, make sure that when you stop at different floors, you stop together.
   2. Elevators can go fast or slow. If you are alone you can work at your own speed; but if you are with others, you have to move and stop in the same rhythm.

SOLUTIONS
Individual children start at "basement" with various floor positions (for example, curled up in ball which unfolds, crouching low with flexed knees and slowly rising; crouching with hands on floor and rising directly to "top" floor; or pausing and holding positions at various levels in between).

Partners stand side by side, shoulders touching; stand face to face, without touching; face with arms extended at shoulders with fingertips touching; stand in wide stride with arms extended, hands touching (rising and descending). (Children's responses: To have people "inside" the elevator who get out at various floors.)

   3. Now we have a new problem. Divide yourselves into small groups and decide who will be the "elevators" and who will be the "passengers." The "elevators" must find a shape that will hold the "passengers" so that you can all move up and down smoothly.
   4. How will you know at what floor someone wants to get out? (Children's responses: The "elevators" will announce the floor at each level, or the "passengers" will call out their floor as a signal to stop.)

ADDITIONAL ELEMENTS   *Creating an external space by relating body shapes; accommodating to tempo and rhythmic pattern; relating to another's movement on different levels.*

Both problems involve an awareness that force *is expended in various ways in moving in or through space (that is, weight must be shifted to different body parts to allow for movement in different directions).*

Children are shaping their outside space (walls, elevators) as well as designing their inside space by stopping at different levels.

The response to elements of size, shape, weight of imaginary objects requires the redistribution of body weight and affects the type of movement in and through space.

The imagery is simple and familiar and can be used as the basis of other activities suggested by the children.

Problem III: To relate levels in space to levels of tone on percussive instruments by responding to accompaniment cues.

A. *There are levels of tone on different instruments that sound high–medium–low just as there are levels in space.*

1. Listen as I play clusters of notes up and down the keyboard; say "high," "medium," or "low" as you hear the levels change.
   [Piano is used as an example but a xylophone may be used, as well as a combination of drum (low), tone block or maracas (middle), and bells or triangles (high).]
2. Move on the same levels that you hear on the piano. When I stop, you stop at the level you hear; when I play, you move again.
3. I may play only at one level or the levels may move up and down; listen to the changes and use your whole body in space.
   (To stimulate a flow of movement from one level to another, chords, clusters, or melodic line are played in an up-and-down progression so that children are constantly changing levels.)
4. This time I'm going to play faster and slower; as you move, feel the rhythm in your muscles so that your bodies will know when the levels change.
   [Accompaniment must have a steady beat with clearly defined measures (that is, 4/4 time in phrases of two or four measures).]

SOLUTIONS

Children's ability to coordinate their movements in relation to a rhythmic pattern and a pitch level varies markedly in the beginning; children may not always stop at the end of a phrase or at a suggested level; initially, movements in response to a particular level may be random and jerky rather than fluid and controlled.

5. Now that you know how it feels to move in space, let your body reach out on different levels; listen to the tone and begin from that level (you may be starting from low, high, or medium).

SOLUTIONS

At middle register, upper part of torso bends forward, swinging from side to side while walking in a forward direction; as register moves toward high, arms elevate and body moves in stretched position walking on tiptoes; from high to low, torso lowers, knees flex, walking in low crouching position, arms swinging at sides.

6. Just as the levels change, the rhythm is going to change, so let your ears listen while your body moves.

SOLUTIONS

Rhythmic changes from 4/4 to 3/4 or 6/8 time produce swinging, swaying, turning, or other body movements; "swinging" rhythms increase range of arms and other body parts; more use of sideward and circular directions in and around each other.

Problem IV: To explore surrounding space on many changing levels in relation to each other.

A. *As you move in and through space, stop on a level that is different from someone near you.*

1. Let's work in small groups of three or four; move together and "pick up" the beat of the drum; when the drum stops, each of you "freeze" at a different level.
[Accompaniment must establish a clear rhythmic pattern (for example, walking, running, swinging, skipping, galloping) through the repetitive, uneven beat in skipping or galloping, the accented beat in 3/4 or 4/4 time, a consistent number of measures in a phrase, and the number of phrases.]
2. Take enough space for yourself but stay close enough together so that you can see whom you are near and at what level to "freeze."

IV.A.1

IV.A.2

IV.A *Solutions: first group*

IV.A *Solutions: third group*

IV.A *Solutions:*
fourth group

3. If you find that you are on the same level as someone else in your group, quickly change and relate your body shape to theirs.

SOLUTIONS

First group. *High:* body stretches with arms raised in open diagonal position over head; *medium:* crouches on both feet, knees flexed, arms extended forward; *low:* torso contracts, arms grasp under legs, head tucked in.

Second group. *High:* torso erect with hands clasped together over head; *medium:* body tilts slightly sidewards, stands with knee flexed on one foot with back leg raised, both arms bent at elbows; *medium:* kneels on back leg, torso rests on back heel, front leg stretched forward, arms at sides; *low:* sitting on floor with arms and legs spread at sides.

Third group. *Low:* body crouched forward, with weight on toe of flexed knee, back leg stretched with weight on toes, hands forward on floor; *medium:* body crouched forward, both knees flexed with weight on front foot, arms contracted toward body, head facing floor; *medium:* legs open wide with knees flexed, torso bent forward through knees, arms stretched upward behind shoulders, head bent toward floor.

Fourth group. *High:* body stretched, legs in wide fourth position, arms stretched from shoulders on the diagonal; *medium:* three children balancing on one leg, with knee flexed, torso bent over flexed knee, back leg stretched backward, arms curved from shoulders, each behind the other in a line at a slightly different level.

Fifth group. *High:* torso erect, with legs in wide second position, arms parallel to legs; *medium:* walks on knees and stops in this position; *medium:* stops on one foot, torso bends forward, with arms held close to middle of body; *low:* full weight on front foot, knee flexed, back leg raised, body supported by both hands on floor.

Sixth group. *High:* body stops in swinging motion, pulling to one side, with weight on one leg, arms extended in parallel arc over head; *high:* stands perfectly still with arms at side, feet slightly apart balancing on toes; *low:* body resting on flexed knee on floor, back leg extended, elbows flexed resting on floor, palms up.

There are two elements of spatial awareness: children must be conscious of the changing levels within the group and they must respond individually by finding their own level and position distinct from any other child. How do children observe and relate to the group as a whole and still express their own quality of movement?

This problem extends an awareness of external and internal space (that is, the space around them formed by relating to other moving bodies and the space which a child creates in finding his own level).

Introduction of time (expressed through tone and rhythm) as well as space and force (that is, each group responds to the tempo and underlying beat but each child develops his own rhythmic pattern as he seeks a level in space).

Finding a level in relation to another body shape elicits increased use of arms, legs, and torso for greater range and differentiation of body parts.

Increased use of directional space (that is, toward, away, in, up, around).

Explorations in Range

Problem I: To explore the extent to which movement reaches out from the body into space.

A. *Any movements that you make in space can be wide or narrow, or large or small.*

1. Let's begin with your own body; even when you breathe, parts of you get larger or smaller and use more or less space.
2. Sit on the floor "Indian style" and rest your hands in your lap.
3. The whole upper part of you is a balloon; start as a very small balloon and fill up with air until you feel your chest and stomach grow larger and larger; hold it until it almost bursts, then let the air out slowly.
4. This time, let's hear the sound of the air going in as the balloon gets bigger, and let's hear it coming out as the balloon gets smaller.

SOLUTIONS
Sounds of "shushing" in through the teeth or lips and "whooshing" out intensifies the breathing movement and increases the range; initially, the "balloon" tends to expand only in the chest cavity in an up-and-down motion.

5. Let's make the balloon even bigger; fold your arms lightly across your stomach so that your elbows are touching your sides; as you fill up with air, fill your whole upper part (not just your chest) and see how far your arms are pushed forward. Do it several times and look at the shape of your body.
6. The balloon can be wider and rounder; rest your hands in your lap but let your elbows touch your sides. When you blow up the balloon, try to make it so wide that it pushes your arms easily away from your sides; as the balloon goes down, let your arms come back slowly.
7. The air in the balloon is going to push your arms out into space; let your arms rise slowly as the balloon gets bigger and bigger and feel how much space your body uses.

SOLUTIONS
Sitting with crossed legs, impulse of breathing in expands chest cavity and lifts arms up and out above shoulders while pulling knees away from floor; inhaling air expands both chest cavity and rib cage, forcing arms out to sides in downward curves;

breathing out carries torso forward over crossed legs, arms arch out and downward until hands rest on floor.

ADDITIONAL ELEMENTS *Rhythmic pattern is introduced by breathing; changes in range produce different body shapes; flow and control of energy affect range of body parts.*

B. *Just as you can change the size of parts of your body, so you can make your whole body bigger or smaller, skinny or wide.*

    1. Your whole body is a balloon; begin from any position (standing, sitting, kneeling) and fill up the balloon from the center of your body (that is, your belly button). As your balloon gets rounder and wider, what happens to your arms and legs and head?

    2. As you reach for space, can you feel the shape of a balloon? What shape are you?

SOLUTIONS

Impulse (breath) from the center of the body pushes the arms and legs outward with greater range of space between limbs and between limbs and torso; attempts are to find round shapes (for example, enclose torso with arms and head bent at middle level; extend arms and legs with a high body stretch; crouch with legs in wide second position, arms stretched at side in downward curve).

    3. You know how a balloon crumples when all the air goes out? Feel the size of your balloon change as you let the air out; begin from where you are now and collapse very slowly.

    4. Now let the air out quickly and feel the difference between being big and small, wide and skinny.

SOLUTIONS

Contrasts in range move from high to low, big to small, wide to narrow (flat); each child moves at different tempo (changes in sustained quality most difficult to control); increased extension of energy increases body range (for example, "crumpled" shapes range from lying flat with whole body pressed into the floor to lying in curled positions on back, side, or stomach).

Problem II: To explore how range of movement is affected by the amount of surrounding space.

A. *When you have lots of space around you, you can make your bodies big or little, wide or narrow. Now explore your movements when you have only a little bit of space.*

1. This whole dance area is a forest. Some of you will be trees; some of you will move through the forest around the trees (two alternating groups).
2. The trees can arrange themselves in different places, with only a small amount of space between each other, but leave enough space for people to move through.
3. Remember that trees have different shapes and sizes, so find a level and shape and hold your position so that the people moving can see the spaces before they come in.
4. The range of your body in space should tell us whether your tree is tall, thick, skinny, small, gnarled, or leafy.

SOLUTIONS
Trees as static objects use elements of space and force (that is, standing, kneeling, lying on different levels with different body parts extended in space). Body shape is determined by the distribution of weight.

B. *As you change groups, feel the difference between the amount of space you use when you do not move and when you move in a small space.*

1. Let us have the moving group start out from different directions and find ways of moving through the small spaces around the trees; start with an easy walk and make sure that you move around every tree.
2. Because the trees are so close together, this time walk between them, slowly stretching whatever part of your body you need to get through.
3. The size of your movements have changed from when you were just walking; what parts of your body are you using now in such little spaces?

SOLUTIONS
Long body stretches to get through a "skinny" space; stretching with arms and shoulders to get under a tree at middle level in space; extending legs to walk over a fallen tree; contracting body with arms pulled in to move through a low, small space.

C. *Now feel the difference in your movements when you walk through more open spaces.*

1. Let's have the trees move out into space and take new positions so that the people can move more freely in different directions with wider and bigger movements.
2. Now let's make uneven spaces; some trees arrange themselves close together, some far apart.

3. In this new forest the moving group can use many different ways of getting through the spaces in as many directions and levels as possible.
4. Now slow down your movements and use more of your body (torso, arms) to move from tree to tree.

SOLUTIONS

Children initially use familiar locomotor movements (for example, walking, running, skipping, and need to be encouraged to move in sideways, backward, and circular directions). Decreasing tempo and emphasizing body movements encourages greater range of body parts and more differentiated use of the body in varying amounts of space.

D. *Each movement we make takes a different amount of space. Explore how much distance you can cover with different parts of your body.*

1. We are out of the forest and you are walking in a stream; some of the stones are very large, some are very small.
2. Step over the small stones across the whole stream. Is there much distance between your legs? What parts of your body are you using?
3. Now the stones are much larger. Can you just step over them or do you need another kind of movement? (Children's responses: Jumping, leaping.)
4. Yes, jumping and leaping use more distance and take you further into space. What other parts of you help to get you across?
5. Now these big and little stones are all mixed up and they are not in a straight line; they are all over the stream; show by the way you move whether you are stepping over big or little stones and where they are in the stream.

SOLUTIONS

Contrasts in range from walking in small steps with body erect on feet or tiptoes over "small" stones to higher and wider movements in jumping and leaping over "large" stones; as distance between legs increases and as each movement is extended, there is greater use of arms for balance, knees are more flexed, torso increases its range in space.

UNDERSTANDINGS FOR TEACHERS—PROBLEMS I–II

How do children express verbally and kinesthetically the changes in their range of movements given more or less space? How do

they become aware that different parts of the body have different ranges of movement?

The static group becomes part of the spatial environment as in a stage setting (that is, the moving group relates to them as "props" whose positions and shapes affect the amount of space available for movement).

Range as a dimension includes space, time, and force [for example, moving from bigger to smaller (or vice versa) involves changes in tempo as well as changes in the flow and control of energy].

Problem III: To explore contrasts in range using animals as imagery.

A. *Animals in the zoo are all sizes and their movements take different amounts of space. What are the largest animals you have seen? (Children's responses: Elephant, giraffe, hippopotamus.)*

1. Choose your animal. Let your movements show whether you are wide and heavy, tall and thin, or tall and wide.
2. Take space out on the floor. An elephant and hippopotamus are both big but they move very differently; feel the difference in the shape of your body and the way certain parts of you move in space.
3. If you are a giraffe, how do you move on long, skinny legs and how does your neck stretch out from your body? Do you move faster or slower than an elephant? How far can your legs take you in space?

B. *What is the smallest animal you have seen in the zoo? (Children's responses: Snake, bird, bat, turtle.)*

1. Whatever small animals you choose, move on different levels, at different speeds, and use different parts of the body.
2. For example, how does a snake use its body when it moves? Do all parts move at once?
3. Where do small animals live? On what do they move (air, earth, water)?

SOLUTIONS

Initial explorations of differences in size of large and small animals tend to result in literal, "storybook" movements; awareness comes from focusing on different qualities of movement in different body parts (for example, stretching, undulating, fluttering, slithering, stomping); from various types of locomotor movements (for example, crawling, striding, flying, wiggling); and from contrasts in distribution of body weight.

UNDERSTANDINGS FOR TEACHERS—PROBLEM III

Whereas imagery involves space, time, and forces, range is emphasized through the qualities of size, weight and shape. (For example, does an elephant have the same range of movement as a snake?) How does the use of space differ in terms of direction, level, tempo? How does range of movement differ in animals who live on the ground, walk on the ground, or fly in the air?

Imagery such as this is familiar and easily adaptable to other sources which include all living and moving things.

Explorations in Focus

Problem I: To explore focus as a means of orientation for direction in space.

A. *What does it mean to "look where you're going"?*

1. Line up so that you can move across the floor, one at a time, in a diagonal direction.
2. Before you move, focus your eyes on me and keep looking as you run; keep your arms out so you can grasp my hands quickly and stop at the end of the line. (Teacher sits, crouches, kneels, stands at the opposite end of the diagonal, with arms outstretched.)
3. What do you see in this room? Take a walk around and look at things; when you hear the signal on the drum, run back here and sit in a group.
4. What did you see? (Children's responses: Windows, blackboard, lights, bookcase, toy shelves, bulletin board.)
5. Divide into four groups; each group will move to some of the things you have seen and the drum will tell you how fast or slow to go, so listen first, then move; when you get there, stay there.

   First group. Window! (Very slow—drum beats heavy, slow 4/4 time.)
   Second group. Blackboard! (Moderate—uneven skipping beats.)
   Third group. Bookcase! (Fast, staccato beat, 4/4 time.)
   Fourth group. Door! (Very fast running beat, 3/8 time.)

6. This time set your own tempo; each person in a group will name a place and the group will move in your rhythm and in your direction. (Each child in a group takes turns giving commands; teacher picks up rhythm on drum or other instrument.)

B. *When you go from place to place, your body may change its usual frontward position and your eyes may have to change too.*

1. Everyone come back and stand perfectly still; find a corner of the room that you want to move to; focus your eyes on it and move slowly toward it; follow your own direction in space and be aware of people around you.
2. From where you are, look at another corner; focus on it and

explore another way of getting there other than moving frontward; when you have touched all four corners, come back and sit down.

SOLUTIONS

Most frequent responses are in frontal locomotor movements (for example, walking, running, skipping, leaping); alternatives include sliding sideways, with head parallel to shoulder and walking backward, with eyes looking over one shoulder.

ADDITIONAL ELEMENTS *Changing body plane (that is, direction that the body faces), tempo, spatial awareness of other moving bodies).*

UNDERSTANDINGS FOR TEACHERS — PROBLEM I

Having children report on their own observations makes them aware of things in the environment and of how directly their bodies can move toward those things through space.

Focus in this problem helps children to become acquainted with the room, to recognize spatial boundaries, and to establish their own tempo level as related to their directional intent.

Problem II: To explore ways in which the direction of the gaze affects movement.

A. *What happens to your sense of balance when you look in one direction and move in another?*

1. Skip across on the diagonal one at a time; begin with your eyes over one shoulder, when you are half way across, shift your eyes to the other side and continue skipping forward (Teacher picks up each child's tempo; emphasizes the beat at which the focus changes.)
2. Now listen to the rhythm of the drum; each time you hear a loud beat, quickly change your focus and come across. (Teacher plays two measures of six beats, accents first beat of each measure.)
3. How many skips did you take before you changed your head? Let's do it again.
4. This time let's change even more quickly; at each loud beat, move your head in another direction. (Teacher beats six measures of 3/4 time accenting first beat of every measure so that the gaze shifts six times.)
5. How many times did your eyes change? What happens to

your sense of direction when you move from here to there changing your focus?

ADDITIONAL ELEMENTS *Relation of accent and focus; response to metrical rhythm and accented beat; awareness of measures and phrasing; introduction of force as greater need for balance.*

B. *Your body acts one way when you "look and move," now let us see how it feels when you "move and look."*

1. Instead of just skipping, come across the floor in twos and threes with a skip and skip and turn and turn pattern. (Uneven rhythmic pattern is the same but the movements change on every measure:

♩♪ ♩♪ / ♩♪ ♩♪ /
skip skip / turn turn / .)

2. Where do your eyes focus when you skip? Where does your body take your eyes when you turn? Where are you looking each time?

3. Now let's see if you can "look where you're going" while you are turning. Come across in twos and threes again and set your own tempo (fast, medium, or slow).

SOLUTIONS

Children relate easily to the general rhythmic pattern of skipping and turning and the turns take different directions; initially, head follows the body but eyes move in a random manner and do not focus as the body returns to a forward direction; in turning too quickly or too slowly, children lose a sense of balance (that is, control of the movement and its direction), which results in staggering and collapsing.

4. You should not have to fall down; this time find your own special point on the wall and try to look at it each time you turn around.

5. Now join hands and make your own "skipping and turning" dance.

UNDERSTANDINGS FOR TEACHERS—PROBLEM II

Any kind of locomotor movements (simple or in combinations) toward a given point in space help children understand that balance and control of their bodies are closely related to their ability to focus; on a simple level, it is understood in terms of looking or not looking where they are going.

As an element of direction, focus is expressed as the direction of the gaze which initiates or accompanies the movement, the plane of the body leading the movement, and the direction in space.

Problem III: To explore the body as the point of reference of focus.

A. *Different parts of your body can lead you into space when you focus on them.*

1. What parts of your body can make movements alone in space? (Children's responses: Feet, legs, head, hands, arms.)
2. Let's explore one part all together, then each of you can focus on a different part and see where it takes you.
3. Sit in a comfortable position and hold up one arm; look at it and move it slowly in curved shapes, in and out, up and down, and around, like the long neck of a swan or an elephant's trunk.
4. Let your arm travel up in space and as you focus on it, let your body rise with it.
5. Now let it lead you *in* space on different levels; keep the movement slow and curved and let the shape of your body follow the shape of your arm.

SOLUTIONS
Children use many of the elements of space; that is, *level*, head follows in parallel position to hand (low-medium-high), line of body follows spatial position of arm; *path*, curved or circular; *range*, larger and small movements, greater or lesser use of space; *body shape*, formed by the internal space between the arm and the body and the shape of the movement in external space; slow, sustained quality produces swinging, swaying, spiraling, and circular body movements.

B. *Focusing on parts of your body can also lead you in different directions through space.*

1. Extend your arm out to the side (left or right) and focus on the tips of your fingers; your body is like a wheel and your fingertips are the center; walk around your hand in six steps and come back to the place where you began; you should be facing the same way.
2. Put your other arm out, focus on the center, and trace the movement of the wheel in six steps. (Drum accompaniment may support the rhythm.)

3. Now put them together, first one hand, then the other, and focus on your fingertips as the center of your space changes.
4. In what directions are you moving? Does your body change its position as you go around? When you combine the movements, what kind of pattern are you making in space?

SOLUTIONS

Children's ability to complete the pattern in six steps varies (exploration is necessary with and without accompaniment). Direction is circular and the body is always frontal; alternating focus from side to side designs a figure-8 pattern.

5. This time let the side of your body follow the focus of your eyes; as you turn, tilt your body in that direction; your movement will be smoother because your whole body is focusing now.

ADDITIONAL ELEMENTS   *Force, redistribution of body weight as center of gravity changes with alternating directions; rhythmic pattern; body plane.*

UNDERSTANDINGS FOR TEACHERS—PROBLEM III

Focus involves all the elements of space–time–force. Space: direction, level, range, pattern, body shape; time: rhythmic pattern, relation to accented beat, to changes in measures and phrases; force: direction of the gaze relates to balance and detracts or reinforces the amount of control necessary for the execution of a movement.

Explorations in Body Shape

Problem I: To explore the body as a three-dimensional object made up of volumes in space.

A. *Your body is a shape that takes up space even when you are standing or sitting still.*

1. Everyone find a place on the floor and sit down in a relaxed position; look at all the different shapes that your bodies make; walk around each other (in small, alternating groups) and see that we have one shape from the front, another from the side, the back, and still another from the top.
2. The way you place your arms, legs, and head in relation to your body makes an "inside" shape; as soon as you move a part of you outward, your body makes a different shape in the "outside" space.
3. Pull every part of you in toward the middle and see what happens to the "inside" space; now extend different parts into the "outside" space, from both a sitting and standing position.

B. *Let's explore different shapes that the body can make.*

1. Make every part of your body as sharp (angular) as it can be. Where are the corners of your body?

   SOLUTIONS
   a. Standing with feet apart, knees flexed outward, elbows flexed parallel to knees with hands toward center of body.
   b. On a low level in space, both knees flexed, weight on back knee and big toe, front leg forward, elbows flexed—one up, one down—fingertips touching in front of face.
   c. Weight suspended between flexed knees and elbows on floor, body in forward position with straight back, forearms crossed with palms facing upward.
   d. Legs in wide stride in diagonal position, with knees slightly flexed, torso bent over forward leg, front arm parallel to leg, back arms flexed at elbow in right-angle position.
   e. Lying on back, with knees flexed, feet on floor, elbows bent, and hands pointing toward knees.

2. How does a circle feel? What is the shape of the space around you? How round can you be?

SOLUTIONS

    a. Standing position, with legs together and arms in circle over head.

    b. Standing position, with legs in wide stride, knees slightly flexed, arms in downward curve at sides.

    c. Crouching position, with knees flexed, torso bent forward, arms in wide arc around head, facing downward.

    d. Standing position, with torso bent forward, head down at knee level, one knee slightly flexed with weight on ball of foot, arms downward in open circle.

    e. Sitting on floor, with legs and arms stretched forward in arc position and neck flexed so that head is parallel to arms.

3. Design the space inside and around you to make a triangle shape; you can be one big triangle or different parts of your body can make little triangles.

SOLUTIONS

    a. Standing with legs in wide stride and arms over head, with flexed elbows, fingers touching in upward point.

    b. Standing on one leg, knee of other leg flexed, with foot resting on inside of straight leg, arms flexed at elbows one above the other across the torso.

    c. Kneeling, weight on flexed knee and big toe of forward foot, other leg resting on ball of foot with knee flexed in outward position, one arm flexed at elbow across the stomach, other arm flexed at elbow points toward head.

ADDITIONAL ELEMENTS   *Level, range, force (tension).*

C. *Now feel the difference in the space as you change from one shape to another.*

1. Begin from whatever shape you like; do not tell us, show it with your body; start from any position—standing, sitting, kneeling, lying, and so on.

2. When you find a shape, change it slowly, slowly into a different shape; can you see that every part of you makes its own shape as you move from one to another?

SOLUTIONS

Some geometric shapes are developed from the previous problems (for example, circles, squares, triangles, rectangles); some begin with abstract shapes which are elaborated into further abstractions.

I.B.2d

I.C.1

3. Those of you who are circular or curved, sharpen your corners and find a square shape; if your shape has angles, soften the movement into a round shape; if you grow from a triangle into a rectangle, feel the stretch in your back, arms, and head.
4. What happens to the shape of the space under your arms when you change? What happens to the space between your legs as you change from a triangle or circle to a tall, skinny rectangle?

UNDERSTANDINGS FOR TEACHERS—PROBLEM I

Children become conscious of not only being *a shape but of* making *a shape, both of which use internal and external space.*

Creating different shapes and changing from one to another makes children aware of the ways different body parts move in space, and with distinctive qualities, for example, soft (round, curved) and sharp (angular, pointed). Beginning with geometric shapes helps to relate the body to shapes of objects in the environment.

Problem II: To explore the relationship of two bodies designing a shape.

A. *Your body can create shapes that have the qualities of objects; can you form the shape of a box?*

1. Take space on the floor; you can work from any position and on any level.
2. We should be able to tell whether it is tall or wide, big or small, flat or bulging, by the way you enclose the space.

SOLUTIONS
a. Kneeling on floor, with weight on flexed knees, torso bent forward from hips, head touching knees, arms at side on floor.
b. Lying on back, with knees maximally flexed and arms enencircling legs.
c. Sitting on floor, back erect, knees flexed and turned out so that soles of feet are touching each other, arms curved in front of torso at shoulder height in a circular shape.
d. Lying on back, in same position as above except legs are bent and elevated, with soles of feet touching, and hands grasping ankles.

e. Sitting on floor, with legs extended parallel in front of body, toes flexed up, arms extended at shoulders parallel to legs.

f. Crawling position on hands and knees, legs slightly apart, hands on floor.

B. *How do you make a box with another person?*

1. Find a place with your partner. Make a box that has both an inside and an outside shape.
2. You do not have to close all the corners or angles; we can see the shape from the spaces in between.

SOLUTIONS

a. Seated, facing each other with legs wide apart, knees straight, arms extended parallel to legs from shoulders, hands and feet touching each other.

b. Standing, with feet in wide position, facing each other, torsos bent forward from hips, backs slightly arched, with arms fully stretched from shoulders; holding hands.

c. Kneeling and facing each other, with arms stretched from shoulder level; holding hands.

d. One partner lying flat on floor, with arms at sides. Other child straddles partner, with legs on each side of body, weight on hands and ball of foot, facing downward, knees and arms straight, with back flat or slightly arched.

e. One child lying on back with legs together and elevated; partner, in standing position behind his head, leans forward, extends arms, and touches partner's feet.

C. *This time make the shape of a box with four people working together.*

1. Feel each other's weight so that you can hold the shape.
2. Your box may be open or closed, and it may have a top; it can stand at any level in space.

SOLUTIONS

a. Standing, with legs apart and arms at side extended at shoulder level; holding hands to form a square shape.

b. Same position as above except that heads bend in and out to "open" and "close" box.

c. Sitting on floor facing center, with legs extended forward and together, arms extended in diagonal position, with elbows flexed (corners) to form square.

d. Lying in prone position each child forms one side of box,

II.B.2b

II.B.2d

II.B.2d

II.C

II.C.2d

II.C.2f

facing down; two "sides" extend arms, touching arms and feet of other "sides" to close corners (shape is created by floor pattern rather than body shape).

e. All standing erect facing inward, two children with weight on one foot, other leg extended sideways and held by other two "sides"; (shape is formed by elevated legs and torsos).

f. "Front" and "back" children standing erect facing outward, each holding a "side" child by one arm and leg. Body weight is supported by other arms and legs (shape is formed by relation of torsos and extended arms and legs).

ADDITIONAL ELEMENTS   Body parts: *Use of body parts alone and in relation to torso, for example, legs and arms, arms and head, trunk, head and arms;* force: *distribution of body weight;* space: *levels, range.*

UNDERSTANDINGS FOR TEACHERS—PROBLEM II

Making a shape first in relation to their own bodies and then in relation to another's sharpens children's kinesthetic awareness of the body's position in space.

New elements of force are brought into being. That is, how does a child feel when he creates a box whose "sides" are supported by others? How does he control his body weight?

Through the simple image of a box children are exploring qualities of shapes (for example, heavy, light), and as they relate this visual–kinesthetic experience to their own body shape, they are abstracting a conventional, everyday object into movement terms.

Problem III: To explore spatial relationships created by group shapes.

A. *Explore a shape where you are touching or connecting with each other.*

1. Even when you close the spaces in between, each body will have its own shape.
2. Work with partners or in small groups.
3. Feel the difference between leaning on someone and just touching them. What happens to your balance?
4. Work at different levels and fill in the space around, under, and over.

III.A.5a

5. You will be meeting and staying together like "frozen" shapes.

SOLUTIONS

a. (Partners.) Sitting on floor facing each other, both with knees flexed and feet on floor. One partner with legs extended in diagonal position encloses other child's legs; heads are downward and touching; arms grasp each other's shoulders.

b. (Partners.) Standing side by side, with weight balanced on one leg, other leg slightly lifted off floor, arms raised and flexed at elbows, inside elbows touching.

c. (Trio.) First and second child sitting on floor, with backs touching, knees flexed, feet on floor, hands on each other's heads; third child sitting, with knees flexed in same position, facing second child, with elbows on his knees.

d. (Trio.) Two children standing in wide lateral stride, side by side, with both inside legs crossed, torsos curved forward, inside shoulders pressed against each other, both holding crossed arms of third child lying on back on floor with hips elevated and legs extended forward through supporting arms of partners.

B. *Each time you make a shape with another person or with a group, the space around you changes.*

    1. Divide in small groups and explore movements that take you *over* and *under* each other.

    2. Are you touching, or are there spaces between you?

    3. Is everyone in your group on the same level in space?

    4. Are you moving and staying together, or are you meeting and moving apart?

SOLUTIONS

a. *Under.* (Trio.) Two children sitting on floor, facing each other, with weight supported by hands placed behind them,

III.A.5d

III.B.4a

legs elevated in diagonal position, knees slightly flexed, each other's soles of feet touching; third child crawls on elbows and knees under arc of feet.

b. *Under.* (Trio.) Two children on floor, with torsos and heads curved downward in opposite directions, weight on one knee and hand, other leg of each child extended back with each other's feet touching; third child drags torso by hands under stomach of each child alternately (in and out).

c. *Over.* (Partners.) One child lying with back on floor, elbows flexed, hands above head, one leg stretched sideward on floor, other leg extended upward in space; partner standing in wide forward stride, with torso bent forward at waist, head down, arms fully extended over elevated leg (almost a suspended fall).

d. *Over.* (Group of four.) Two children facing in crouched position on floor, with weight between hands and toes; third child standing between them, weight on one leg, other leg

III.B.4b

III.B.4c

III.B.4d

IV.A
Group shape

elevated to side with knee highly flexed, steps sideways over backs of crouching children. Fourth child follows third in circular pattern.

ADDITIONAL ELEMENTS *Range of movement, spatial direction in relation to body plane, levels, balance and control of body weight.*

Problem IV: To form one group shape through the interrelationship of individual body shapes.

A. *You can make a large group shape if you design your own body in relation to others around you.*

   1. Divide into groups of fives or sevens; find a place on the floor and work together to develop your shape; then we will look at them separately.
   2. Let's have a person in each group create the first shape, and each of you, one at a time, find a shape that relates to it; take turns making the first shape.

3. Work in all levels and directions—below, above, around, behind, and in front of each other.
4. We should be able to see two kinds of space, the space around your own body shape and the space that you create between each other.

SOLUTIONS

(Group shapes are demonstrated facing the observers in relation to what is defined as the "front" of the dance area.)

First child, facing sideways, with legs in wide frontward stride, arms extended from shoulders, with hands curved downward and head between arms, facing floor.

Second child, standing behind first child, with legs in lateral stride, upper torso bent at waist in forward position, front arm extended forward, back arm resting on thigh, and head extended, facing downward.

Third child, standing, facing first child on the diagonal, with legs in lateral stride, back arm extended from shoulder almost touching hands of first child, making a circular shape, front arm on downward curve, facing floor.

Fourth child, facing forward, with torso bent at waist under arms of first and third children, legs in open forward stride, front arm extended in downward curve, facing downward.

Fifth child, standing beside and slightly in front of second child, with legs in lateral stride, torso bent forward from waist, inside hand curved downward almost touching extended arms of fourth child, with head at same level but not touching.

Sixth child, crouching on floor, with both knees flexed, weight between inside knee and foot of outside leg, torso curved forward with head resting on raised knee, front hand extended in downward position, other arm stretched backward between legs of first and fourth child.

Seventh child, lying on floor facing toward center, with torso flexed from hips folded over front bent knee, back leg fully extended, arms curved on floor with elbows flexed, head down.

5. What was the shape of your group? (Children's responses: curved, circular, triangular, free-formed.)
6. What was the general shape of each person's body within it? Was it the same as the large group shape?
7. This is not "follow the leader." You are meeting and surrounding each other using your bodies in different ways.

IV.A *Solutions: first child*

IV.A *Solutions: second child*

IV.A *Solutions.*
third child

IV.A *Solutions:*
fourth child

UNDERSTANDINGS FOR TEACHERS—PROBLEMS III–IV

Children discover that when they work in relation to others they are not only creating their own body shapes, but are becoming part of new spatial relationships.

Creating shapes involves various spatial dimensions (up–down, in–out, under, around, far–near) and directional elements (in front of, behind, beside) allow children to explore the limitations and possibilities of each particular body shape.

IV.A *Solutions:*
fifth child

IV.A *Solutions:
sixth child*

Forming group shapes introduces new spatial relationships which emerge from meeting and moving together, meeting and moving apart, approaching and encircling or surrounding.

Static or "frozen" shapes require greater control of body parts through the distribution of body weight (that is, the difference between interlocking or open shapes involves differences in the flow and control of energy).

Group shapes do not always remain static but may be used in explorations of locomotor movement.

IV.A *Solutions:
seventh child*

9. Concept: time

A child cannot grasp the concept of space unless it is limited and defined; similarly, time as a concept must be divided and made relative in order to be understood. That is, it must be arranged in groupings which have a beginning and an end.

Time is expressed in the body as *rhythm*, which penetrates the body through those functions which are recurrent, such as pulse, heartbeat, breath. A child's inherent rhythm can sometimes be noted by observing him walk across the floor without accompaniment. Frequently the beat that he establishes will have a relationship to his own heartbeat or energy level. Thus, the essence of a child's response to rhythm is a kinesthetic awareness of his underlying pulse, but it is also experienced as a phenomenon of force and time. Through dance explorations children learn that time is more than faster or slower motion; it is deeply connected to their movement expression, for it gives meanings which may alter its entire characteristic.

In its broadest sense, rhythm is movement, and there can be no body motion without rhythm. This does not imply, however, that mere repetition of a movement produces rhythm. A rhythmic pattern is more easily distinguished when there is repetition, but of itself it does not make a movement aesthetically rhythmical. For example, successive repetition of a single movement or an entire movement sequence may lend emphasis and intensity, but so may prolonged repetition make a movement tedious or overextended. Either condition can only be sensed by a child in terms of the quality of expression he is trying to achieve. Thus, repetition is not an element which should be used mechanically, but an expressive function of rhythm which is itself creatively composed. In order to awaken a consciousness of rhythm in children, they must sense the need for cooperation of all the muscles in the body. As they become more aware of their own movement, they come to realize that although an impulse may begin in one part of the body, it affects the action of all of the muscles. It is this kind of awareness which helps children understand that their bodies move as a totality in both time and space.

Dalcroze, whose system of Eurythmics was built on the belief that rhythm is the coordinating element of all human action, defined rhythm as "a series of connected movements forming a whole," whose main characteristics are "continuity and repetition."[1] At the same time he

[1] Emile Jaques-Dalcroze, *Eurythmics, Art, and Education* (New York: A. S. Barnes, 1935), p. 3.

stressed that the kinesthetic response is dependent upon the spontaneous feelings and emotions which initiate the body's movements. We may say, therefore, that rhythm gives structure to the emotions and is a means by which a child organizes and interprets them through movement.

In a specific sense body rhythm is a varied succession of muscular tensions, relaxations, and rests. As metaphorically expressed by H'Doubler, "Rhythm as an experience may be said to be measured energy." [2] Just as children need to discover how to use space expressively, so do they need to internalize ways in which time is used for contrast, accentuation, and physical balance. Children do not necessarily have an instinct for time or time values. This simply means that although all children have an inherent bodily rhythm, they do not all have the same motor faculties; therefore all do not necessarily have rhythmic awareness. Although the ability to perceive and respond to rhythmic patterns varies, such perception is made sharper because rhythm is the very heart of the dance experience.

The extent to which children learn to

develop a rhythmic sense depends largely upon the sensitivity of the teacher, perhaps more in this area than in any other. Children find it difficult to move rhythmically under the guidance of a teacher who does not herself respond kinesthetically (that is, feel pulse, duration, and tempo in her own body). If she can neither "keep time" in terms of setting a beat for children to follow nor discern the rhythmic patterns that they create, she is unable to recognize a similar lack of perception in children. The problem, then, becomes one of not only failing to stimulate their rhythmic acuity, but of actually impeding their awareness. For teachers new to dance, the use of a drum or other percussive instrument may reinforce their own sense of rhythm. By keenly observing the responses of the children, it will soon become apparent whether such accompaniment clarifies or confuses. In this instance, as in all others, teachers can learn from children. A child with a strong feeling for rhythm is usually eager to provide a simple, percussive accompaniment or to initiate a rhythmic pattern in movement. (Accompaniment and sound will be discussed at the end of this section.)

As an aesthetic component of dance, rhythm plays an important role in orga-

[2] Margaret N. H'Doubler, *Dance—A Creative Art Experience* (Madison: University of Wisconsin Press, 1968), p. 86.

nizing movements and in giving coherence to the total form. It integrates the various elements of movement by providing a time structure, or grouping of beats, which determines the relative duration and stress of the movements within it. Thus, just as movements create visual patterns in space, so do they create observable patterns in time.

In order to understand these time patterns, it is necessary to be aware that they derive from two sources; from music, where rhythm is produced through sounds, and from dance, where rhythm is created from movements. Thus, in dance time is experienced through both metric and rhythmic patterns. *Metric patterns* come from music and are more familiarly known to us as *tempo, beat, measure,* and *phrasing. Rhythmic patterns* are evoked from internal bodily rhythms and are defined in terms of *pace, pulse,* and *duration.* Although there is a similarity between the two structures, and they are sometimes described interchangeably, dance has its own vocabulary which needs to be clarified.

Perhaps the concept of internal and external rhythm can best help children discriminate between rhythmic and metric time. Internal rhythm is a combination of pulse, heartbeat, and breath that

is brought to bear on the elements of dance whether the impetus is a specific image or an abstract movement problem. It is internal time in the sense that it is self-imposed, and it only functions in relation to the experience of the movement itself. This means that for however long it lasts, it is continuous and all-inclusive. In a fundamental way it is the difference in response between "take an easy walk around the room," in which a child establishes his own tempo and pattern of steps, and "take a walk with the drum," where each step must correspond to a sound or beat. As children learn to coordinate these rhythms, they begin to achieve a kind of physical balance. H'Doubler refers to this as "rhythmic sensations [which] feel right because of the right proportioning of the time and stress values that bind all the related parts into a unified experience sensed as a whole." [3]

A further difference may be drawn between "free rhythm" and "keeping time." In the latter, we are not concerned with being "on time," but "in time," in the sense of responding to a grouping of beats that is based on a mathematically organized structure. External rhythm, therefore, is a response which can be accurately

[3] Ibid., p. 86.

followed in movement by counting. Actual verbal counting while moving, however, is not suggested, for it tends to make a child's consciousness of rhythm cerebral instead of kinesthetic, and frequently it results in movements that are mechanical and unfluid. As a characteristic of metrical time, it is merely a means of explaining that one movement may last half as long as another, or may be two, three, four, or six times as long. By way of definition, then, a metric pattern reflects the relationship between the duration of one movement and that of another.

Thus, time is divided into rhythmic and metric patterns through which it is made functional. To assure that they are not regarded as techniques, however, they must be seen in terms of their aesthetic relationship to the expression of dance itself. While children must experience the elements of rhythm as organized groupings, teachers must understand that children may not always respond to a regular rhythmic pattern, but may improvise patterns of their own. Even with folk music, which children especially enjoy for its simple repetitions and familiar content, the rhythm does not always follow in regular measures, but may change from 3/4 to 4/4 in the middle of the song. We need always to be sensitive to the possi-

bility that a child may respond not to the rhythm that he hears at a given moment, but to the rhythm that he feels.

The question of whether a child is developing rhythmic awareness does not rest solely upon his ability to follow a rhythmic or metric pattern. The crucial question is the following: In getting from one movement to another, what is happening with the body between the beats? Although we are not attempting to produce polished dancers, we are concerned with developing in children a similar feeling for flow and continuity. We might call this phenomenon of "betweenness" the sensuous connective tissue which gives movement its organic quality. Or we may speak in terms of the transition from one movement to the next, which may be observed as fluid and continuous or jerky and mechanical.

Children can appreciate the notion that we do not dance "by the numbers." Whether a child responds to a metrical pattern or to his own rhythm, he is involved in exploration and improvisation of movement qualities. Therefore, it is the unified feeling that his body is able to express which determines whether he is merely executing isolated gestures or is engaged in the total process of dance. Opportunities to move in response to both rhythmic and metric patterns offer alternatives through which he can control his body and broaden the scope of his rhythmic expression.

It is in exploring the elements that make up these basic rhythms that children become aware of how time, which they both create and use, comes into being. Every child, whether he is aware of it or not, has an individual preference for tempo. Changes and contracts in time are partially defined in terms of *tempo* and *pace*. To draw an equation between the two patterns, we may say that tempo is to music what pace is to dance.

Pace is determined by the amount of time it takes to execute a movement from its beginning impulse to the end. Taken more broadly, it refers not only to the rate of speed of a single movement, but to the general tempo level of an entire movement sequence. Pace has much to do with the expression of "movement color," or mood. Although there are no rigid formulas, successive slow movements tend to produce a quality of solemnness, whereas a vigorous tempo may suggest a more vibrant feeling. Whatever mood or emotion a child wishes to express, changes in pace may lend more or less intensity to the quality of the movement.

Although variations in pace are gen-

erally described as fast and slow, there are gradations along this continuum which create subtlety and interest. For example, the pace may be steady and constant or it may be changing and irregular. A simple locomotor or body movement, a brief improvision, or a dance study make take on one appearance if it is performed in a thoroughly unrelieved tempo. Or, as an alternative, the emotional intent or abstract quality of the movement may be completely altered by introducing dynamics (which involve changes in force as well as time), such as fast–slow–fast; slow–fast–slow; or the entire range from slow to fast, fast to slow.

Pace is also marked by changes which are sudden or gradual, not in a random, uncontrolled way, but in keeping with the tempo level that a child sets for himself. There are infinite movement possibilities when the pace is changed through sudden or gradual transitions of movements. Descriptions such as "constant pace with sudden changes; changing pace with gradual changes" or "fast pace with light movements; slow pace with heavy movements" cannot be fully realized in language, for they tend to be regarded as isolated exercises. A child will only sense the effects of these dynamics as he experiments with different rhythmic elements within the context of what he is trying to express.

Characteristics of pace become known to children very directly as they discover that different parts of their bodies function differently in time. They become aware, for example, that partly because of the structure of their muscles and partly because of the placement on the body, the head, legs, arms, hands, feet, and torso can move at different rates of speed. By varying the pace at which each body part moves (alone or in combinations), they can see as well as feel that such changes affect the total time pattern. At this point the rhythmic elements of pulse and duration also come into being as the other essential components of rhythmic patterns.

In metric pattern, *tempo* is the rate of speed of a movement, or the rate at which one movement follows another. The tempo of any movement depends upon *beat*, which is the pulse of music, just as the heartbeat is the pulse of internal rhythm. The difference is that metric patterns derive from an external source of rhythm, *meter*. Through whatever structure is used—3/4, 4/4, 6/8—it is a grouping of beats in mathematical relationships which determines the duration of each beat. Children's rhythmic response in movement may correspond to the number of beats in a measure, the number of measures, or to groupings of measures into phrases.

Tempo, like pace, is continuous and repetitive and defines the intervals of the unit by which time is measured. In rhythmic patterns the interval is sensed as pulse; in metric patterns it is established by beat. Thus, although tempo may be fast, slow, or moderate, it acts as the steady underlying line against which beats form a pattern.

Because rhythm is produced by sounds in music and by movements in dance, we need to understand the difference between these two units of time. Stated simply, *beat* in music is a component of time, while *pulse* in dance functions in both time and force. Beat in itself can be subdivided, but there must be at least two to define an interval in time. Beyond this, other groupings are possible, such as even intervals of 3, 4, 6, or uneven beats such as 5, 7, 9. The latter makes for less symmetrical movement and requires keener rhythmic perception because it departs from traditional metric standards and frequently produces more interesting responses.

We can observe these relative durations in terms of simple locomotor movements.

For example, the walk, as our basic motor activity, corresponds to the basic time unit, which is the quarter note. For this reason the walk serves as the focus for beginning movement exploration; it is a comfortable, everyday experience, requires less control than other steps, and can be easily heard in sound or musical accompaniment. A graphic representation of the relation of beat to movement is shown at the bottom of this page.

In rhythmic patterns pulse also represents an amount of time, but as dance is a kinesthetic experience, it is expressed by the body as greater or lesser force. Each pulse as projected in a movement is an extension of force in a moment of time. Mettler informs us that, "All natural movement is characterized by a continuous flow of impulses, one growing out of another, each distinct and yet continuous with the preceding and following one." [4] In terms of establishing a rhythmic pattern, therefore, every movement impulse represents an alternation of degrees of force, and the greatest amount of force given to a particular movement is felt as a beat.

For further definition, beats are both *accented* and *unaccented*, just as pulse may be *regular* or *irregular*. Accent may be described as emphasis which is heard as louder or softer sounds given to certain beats which occur in a series. There may be any number of beats, depending upon

[4] Barbara Mettler, *Materials of Dance as a Creative Art Activity* (Tuscon, Ariz.: Mettler Studios, 1960), p. 112.

whole note	𝅝	—sustained, very slow walk
half note	𝅗𝅥	—slow walk
quarter note	♩	—walk, natural tempo
eighth notes	♫	—run
eighth notes (triplets)	♫♪ 3	—fast run
uneven beats (eighth and sixteenth)	♪♫ ♪♫	—skip, gallop

the pattern of the movement, but there must be at least two in order for an accent to have meaning. A series of beats without accents is difficult to respond to, whether in sound or music. In any rhythmic activity, including speech, we sense the need to give a continuous grouping of beats differing degrees of emphasis. Thus, an accented beat gives coherence to music as it gives impulse to rhythm. Each accented beat in music and each impulse in dance is a force which produces motion suddenly and immediately. Without them creative movement would be aimless and monotonous.

Children become aware as they respond to metric time that in any grouping of beats, long or short, simple or complex, the starting beat usually receives special emphasis. As they feel the rhythm in their bodies, they begin to separate *metrical accent* from rhythmic accent as an added force that is given to the first beat of every measure. A simple rhythm provides for only one accent, as in 2/4 or 3/4 time, but in 4/4 or 6/8 there may be two accents. In the case of a double accent, the first and second may be of equal force or the first may be stronger. This is a general description, however, and is not invariable when applied to actual movement. For example, although the accent

usually falls on the first beat in 4/4 time, it is conceivable and desirable to design rhythmic experiences wherein accented movements are executed on the second, third, or fourth beat. The same holds for 3/4, or waltz, time, where shifting the accent from the first to the second beat may offer possibilities for interesting and inventive patterns.

An approach toward eliciting more improvisational responses to metrical rhythm offers two alternatives: (1) As long as a child maintains the feeling of the underlying beat, he is free to change the accent to support the meaning and feeling of the movement, yet it cannot be changed in every measure for it would have no structure at all. (2) Metrical or accented beats do not necessarily have to be performed as a "step" on the downbeat. A repeated gesture by one part of the body may indicate an accent, as may a sharp pause or stillness in contrast to vigorous movement.

As an expression of time–force, *pulse* is a regular, recurrent wave of movements which may be likened to the throbbing or rhythmic beat in poetry. The relationship is to that poetry which departs from a standard meter, but has an open form designed only to give emphasis to the emotional intent of the words. In regard to pulse, such emphasis is seen as *stress*, which is the degree of force or intensity expended in a movement. Although pulse reflects an internal rhythmic continuity, stress is applied to a movement for emphasis or clarity. It may be placed on important beats, measures, or phrases, but in any form it is given to a particular movement at a specific time to intensify the quality of that movement. Thus, in responding to an underlying pulse, a child may establish his own rhythmic pattern in which the accent does not fall on the first beat. In this experience he is defining a *rhythmical accent*.

Whether a pulse is regular or irregular depends upon the stress given to a movement. If every pulse is of equal duration in time and is equal in weight or force, the pulse is regular and steady. When seen as a pattern, each movement appears as long as any other. Similarly, if each impulse is given an unequal time–force value, the pulse is irregular. These dimensions occur in relationships which may be expressed as "long" and "short." For example, two or more movements of unequal duration may in themselves create an irregular pulse beat, but if repeated in the same sequence, they become regular. A simple pattern can be diagrammed in both rhythmic and metrical terms as follows:

——— — / ——— — /
long   short   long   short

♩.   ♪   /   ♩.   ♪

long   short   long   short

——— — / ——— —

♩.   ♪   /   ♩.   ♪

(Emphasis determines whether the rhythm is a skip or a gallop.)

By experiencing these time elements in various combinations, children come to realize that a rhythmic structure is made up of certain groupings of beats and accents which they can impose over an underlying pulse. In responding to different groupings kinesthetically, they become aware that accents or stress come into being through movement and that it is these elements which bind a movement sequence together and give it a feeling of unity.

Once we are involved with any grouping of beats around an accent, we are defining a *measure*. By grouping beats into measures we can create more complex and extended movement patterns. Measures may be considered as groupings of like intervals (underlying beat and accents) into larger units of time. Children's experience with verbal expression helps them bridge the notion that a measure is a sentence of the beats, just as a spoken

131

sentence is a line of words. To express this rhythmically, however, they must first discover the underlying pulse, which they can do by responding to the steady beat, and then to each separate beat which forms the melody or "words." Only through direct exploration do they become aware that although the tempo remains the same, the duration of the impulses may be faster or slower, even or uneven.

Searching for appropriate movements to express ways in which different rhythms relate to each other is a richer kinesthetic experience than merely beating time with the hands. Clapping may serve as a "warm-up," but awareness of measure also comes through a consciousness of change and contrast. For example, once the beat has been established changes in measure can be defined by changing direction, introducing dynamics of loud and soft, using larger or smaller movements, and as has been noted, shifting the accent. Whatever elements are used to demonstrate these changes will inevitably alter the space (direction, range, body shape) and force (heavy and light) of the movement pattern.

When measures are formed into larger rhythmic structures, we are concerned with *phrasing*. As a measure is a rhythmic sentence, so a phrase may be considered

a paragraph. Just as we speak in sentences and need to stop for breath, so in music or movement we group time to give the same "rounding off" feeling to our ideas before starting again. Thus, phrasing is a rhythmic sequence of movements which develops and diminishes in the same way that a flowing inflection of the voice gives a sense of partial or total completion at the end of a paragraph.

A phrase is of greater duration than a measure and is a means by which children learn to respond to larger groupings of time. It may be short or long, and although it must have at least two measures, each phrase does not necessarily have to be equal in length. Because its function is to express a continuous movement theme, it is not merely an adding together of measures. The number of measures may be arbitrary, but the need for phrasing depends upon the way time and force values are used as expressive qualities. In movement, as in music, phrasing is that element of time that is organized to give a sense of fluidity and continuity from the beginning to the end of a movement sequence.

When we speak of measures and phrases as divisions of time, these same elements are expressed in dance as *duration*. Every movement has duration which is the span or interval of time from its beginning to the end. In moving to metrical patterns, children become aware that time is divided into groupings which must be related to an underlying beat or meter. That is, the basic rhythm is "given" and it is left to them to design movement within it. Although this is not the same as "real" or clock time, it is structured in the sense that each beat or movement must be given its appropriate time value.

In rhythmic patterns we are dealing with *relative duration,* in which the underlying pulse emerges from the form of the movement itself. Thus, the length of time of a movement is created and lasts only in relation to other movements. The amount of actual or clock time is of no import, for the duration of a movement or a series of movements depends upon the force necessary for its expression and the amount of space necessary for its execution. Therefore, although duration exists in time, it is also a force that is directed and released and that is extended in space.

It is interesting to note that even when there is no external metrical structure, children's movement reflects a need for a unit of measure (perhaps to give some organization to the internal rhythms of the body), for children inevitably produce an underlying pulse. Even when they evolve a rhythmic pattern that they have not consciously defined, we can "pick up" that beat, and frequently, the measures and phrasing. Once a child establishes a unit of time in whatever exploration or improvisation he is engaged, we can then determine the duration of a movement. The extent to which children develop a feeling for duration largely determines their awareness of time patterns.

To add a visual dimension to the concept of time, the forms of rhythmic and metric patterns can be diagrammed to show their relationship. Such schema, however, are only presented for teachers, because it is not recommended that children become involved in learning to move initially from graphic representations. Any rhythmic structure must first be sensed in the body before it can be meaningfully interpreted through musical symbols or pictorial signs. For example, if a child is asked to respond in movement to two measures of four beats, he must "feel" that duration within his body and sense the moment at which to begin the next measure. This is a qualitatively different feeling than if he were to express duration with the same movements while counting "1, 2, 3, 4." The diagrams, therefore, are intended as a general reference

133

METER

Whole note o
Half note ♩
Quarter note ♩
Eighth notes ♫
Sixteenth notes ♬

	4/4 time (four beats to a measure, quarter note gets one beat)				3/4 time (three beats to a measure, quarter note gets one beat)		
Measure	1	2	3	4	1	2	3
METRIC PATTERN							
Slow, even							
Slow, uneven							
Moderate, even							
Moderate, uneven							
Fast, even							
Fast, uneven							
	Underlying pulse: four beats				*Underlying pulse: three beats*		
RHYTHMIC PATTERN							
Slow, even							
Slow, uneven							
Fast, even							
Fast, uneven							

for some of the movement problems included in this chapter, upon which teachers can draw for further elaboration.

Rhythmic patterns can be diagrammed as horizontal lines which denote duration from the beginning of one movement to the beginning of the next. Each line represents a pulse. Seen in succession, the length of a line indicates whether a movement is long or short and whether the pulse is regular or irregular.

Metric patterns are diagrammed in terms of musical notation. The groupings of beats are established by the meter (or time signature, as it is called in music), which determines the number of beats in a measure and the duration of each beat.

In order to draw an analogy between these two time structures, the more familiar patterns of 4/4 and 3/4 time will be used.

Explorations in Rhythmic Patterns

Problem I: To explore rhythm by organizing it into long and short beats.

A. *Each of you uses time differently in dance, and the way you show it is through rhythm.*

  1. If-I-speak-to-you-with-out-chang-ing-my-voice-how-does-it-sound? What is missing? (Children's responses: Flat tone, no tone, all the same, no rhythm.)
  2. Sound and rhythm go together; let's explore the rhythms of your own name.
  3. What is your name? Clap it exactly as you say it; your feet will move to the rhythm your hands clap, and your whole body will move to your name. How are you going to move? (Each child responds in turn.)
  4. As you move across the floor, talk the movements you are making so that you can hear them as well as feel them; be sure to end your movement on the last syllable of your name.
  5. Let's have the whole group talk the movements with you. (Each child moves alone for the first phrase, then teacher or another child picks up the rhythm on the drum.)

  SOLUTIONS
  (Initially there may be a lack of coordination between the verbal and kinesthetic response, for example, two syllables are spoken but three beats are clapped, or more frequently, the reverse occurs. Movements do not always reflect accented beats.)

  a. "Chris - to - pher An - tho - ny John - son" (Claps inaccurately.) Did he clap "John - son" or "John - on - son"? Take it again, Chris. (Chris claps and the group responds.) How will you move to it?

  run   run   run jump jump jump leap leap

  short short short short short short long long

  b. "Doug - las   Ee - yore   Vo - gel"
  (Eeyore, like in Winnie the Pooh?)
  skip   and   skip   and   jump jump

  long   short long   short long long

c.

"Jen - i - fer	Joyce	In - dic - tor"
run run run	run	step leap leap

short	short	short	long	short	long	long

Both legs come off the floor when you leap, don't they? If you take a big step on *Joyce*, it's not a run, it's a leap. Do it again and feel the difference between a long and a short step.[5]

6. How can you use your arms to get bigger movement?
7. Now come across the floor in groups of four, taking turns moving to each one's name. (Accompaniment follows each group's rhythmic pattern.)

B. *Every sentence that you speak has a rhythm of long and short beats; let's put the rhythm of the words and the movement together.*

1. What street do you live on? Say the whole sentence, "I live on _____ _____." When you feel the rhythm, clap it.
2. As we listen to each person, we can hear that some of you have different streets but with the same rhythm.
3. Listen to the drum speak your different rhythms and see if you can tell what street it is. (Teacher may call on children with streets of same and different rhythmic patterns to emphasize similarity and contrast.)
4. Now tell us what street you live on by just clapping the rhythm. (Other children identify the rhythm; group can also create choral rhythms or diverse rhythmic sound patterns.)
5. Come across the floor one at a time on the diagonal. First clap the sentence as you say it, then move to that rhythm.
6. The drum will help you hear the long and short beats; you begin and the drum will follow you.

SOLUTIONS
(Duration of beats corresponds to the syllables of the words.)

a.

"I	live	on	West	Hill	Drive"
leap	leap	leap	run	run	run

long	long	long	short	short	short

[5] These solutions are excerpted from the author's master's thesis, *Creative Rhythmic Movement for Young Children*, UCLA, 1959, pp. 72–77.

b. "I   live   on Wis - con - sin Av - e -nue"
jump jump jump step together step step together step

long long long short short short short short short

c. "I   live   on   Mc - Comb   Street"
run   run   run syncopated step   leap

short short short   short long   long

d. "I   live   on   Thir - ty   Third Place"
leap leap leap stamp stamp stamp stamp
(arms outstretched)

long long long short short short long

e. "I   live   on   I - da - ho Av - e -nue"
crouching with   six runs on
  knees bent   tiptoes

long long long short short short short short short

C. *Now let's put two rhythms together by moving to two names at the same time.*

1. Work in partners; find a rhythmic pattern for each name and move first to one and then the other.
2. Now put the two names together; explore different directions while you are moving in the same space.
3. Repeat the pattern three times; change from one name to the other or use them both together.

SOLUTIONS

a. "Mat - tie Tur - ner"   "Jac - que - line Bec - ler"
step turn step turn   step step step turn turn

long long long long   short short short long long

(Facing each other, moving together from opposite ends of the diagonal; same underlying beat, different rhythm pattern.)

b. "Be - ver - ly"   "Mar - i - lyn"
step together step   step hop hop

long short short   long short short

(Standing side by side; moving forward in forward direction. Same rhythmic pattern.)

c. "Jer - e - my Wal - ton"   "Ted Stein - berg"
   slide step slide walk walk   stride leap   leap

   —   —   —   —— ——   ——   —   —
   short short short long long   long short short

(Standing slightly apart; facing same direction. One moves, then the other. Same underlying beat; different rhythmic pattern.)

4. Use parts of your body other than your feet to "talk" the rhythm; let your arms help you move through space.

ADDITIONAL ELEMENTS *Direction, range, difference in energy expended on long and short beats.*

UNDERSTANDINGS FOR TEACHERS—PROBLEM I

Beginning with a personal reference such as his own name or street, a child becomes aware that the rhythm of his syllables corresponds to rhythmic units of longer or shorter time. Whether he moves accurately to his own sounds demonstrates his kinesthetic response to the pulse that he establishes.

Relating rhythmic patterns to verbal symbols emphasizes the association of sound and rhythm. Each child says his own name until it loses its immediate connotation and becomes a rhythmic pattern. In hearing and observing others, children discover that each name has its own peculiar rhythmic quality or inflection which can be translated in movement terms. When several children respond to the same pattern, each shows a different use of space and force.

The drum in this case serves only to emphasize and reinforce the sound–rhythm relationship established by each child.

Problem II: To explore the relationship of different rhythmic patterns using imagery.

A. *A clock tells time in three ways. What are they? (Children's responses: Hours, minutes, seconds.)*

   1. Your torso is the face of a clock; use only your torso to show hours, minutes, or seconds.

   SOLUTIONS
   Minutes. Swinging back and forth, flexing from the hips.
   Hours. Pivoting in a circle around the hips; turning in place

slowly, with arms extended to sides; bending forward from hips, swinging head, torso, arms in side-to-side motion. *Seconds.* Torso bending forward, bouncing up and down from hips.

2. Using your whole body, show how your clock moves from 12 o'clock, 3 o'clock, 6 o'clock, 9 o'clock, and back to 12 o'clock again.

SOLUTIONS

a. *12 o'clock.* Standing erect, both arms close together bent at elbows, pointing upward in front of face. *3 o'clock.* Right arm extended sideward (left hand remains at 12 throughout). *6:00.* Right arm points downward between legs. *9:00.* Right arm crosses body at waist, points left. *12:00.* Joins left hand in original position.

b. Both hands move together from hour to hour in continuous circle in front of body.

3. Some of you are moving only on the hour; some are moving on every beat; and some are moving in one big circle from hour to hour.

4. Do it again and feel how many beats it takes you to get from one hour to another. Let's look at some of the clocks and hear their "tick-tock." (Teacher picks up each child's beat on some percussion instrument to emphasize different rhythmic patterns.)

5. Some of you are taking four beats, some three. Listen to the rhythm of the drum and change the hour each time you hear a strong beat. (Teacher alternates between 4/4 and 3/4 time to demonstrate different rhythmic patterns and to encourage response to accented beats.)

6. Your movement has a different quality when you use three beats or four beats. Can you feel the difference? What kinds of movements are you making?

SOLUTIONS

3/4 time tends to produce swinging, swaying, circular, or arc-like movement; 4/4 time tends to produce more percussive (striking) movement.

7. Keep one hand on the hour and move the other hand on the minutes; you can move the minute hand anywhere in space. (Teacher alternates between 4/4 and 3/4 time, playing enough phrases of each so that children can sense the difference in movement.)

8. Now change the hour on every fifth beat; feel the five beats

in your body as you hear them. (Teacher plays 5/4 time, accenting the first beat of every measure.)

B. *Let's explore the different rhythms of the minutes and seconds against the steady beat of the hours.*

1. Divide into three groups—hours, minutes, seconds. "Hours," move with your whole body; "minutes," move with your arms; "seconds," use only your legs.
2. Here are some instruments which have sounds like a clock; listen to each one and decide which sounds like hours, minutes, or seconds. (Teacher distributes instruments arbitrarily and children experiment with different sounds and rhythms; children alternate between playing and listening.)
3. Now some of you from each group take the instruments and sit together so you can hear each other; watch your own group very carefully before you play, so that you can pick up your rhythm; let's have the hour establish the steady beat.

SOLUTIONS
Instruments:

hour	𝅝	gong, cymbals, drum
minutes	♩ ♩ ♩ ♩	tone block, tone gourd, maracas
seconds	♫ ♫ ♫ ♫	triangle, bells, claves

(Because children need to listen to each other as well as to relate their sounds to movement, instruments should be played by small groups at a time; for example, one child for the hour, three to four children for the minutes, three to four children for the seconds.)

Movement: Hour: (Sustained movement.) Torso bending from hips, swinging or rocking like a pendulum, side to side; back and forth. Describes a whole circle; slowly turns in complete circle while standing in place; legs in wide lateral stride, steps on alternate feet, with body leaning from side to side on every hour. Turns clockwise in circular direction with one arm extended forward. *Minutes:* One arm is extended sideward and remains still while other arm moves in clockwise direction. Arms move in opposite circles, crossing in front of face. With one arm extended forward, other arm moves in arc above it, from side to side. Arms swing back and forth and from side to side. *Seconds:* Standing and rocking back and forth on alternating feet; stepping side to side on alternating feet; jumping with feet apart and together sideways. Same jumping move-

II.B *Solutions:*
movement

ment with feet forward and backward. Jumping and turning on one foot, other leg jumps from ball of foot, with knee flexed. Sitting, with knees flexed and feet stepping alternately on floor.

ADDITIONAL ELEMENTS Space (body parts): *isolation of torso for large body movements, use of arms and legs separately and in combination;* range *of movement;* force: *sustained and percussive movements.*

4. Take a partner. When you have developed a rhythmic pattern, the people with instruments will pick up your rhythm. (After a period of free exploration, each group improvises before the class.)

Instruments: Hour: drum; *minutes:* claves and tone gourd; *seconds:* triangle and maracas.

Movement:

    a. "Hour" standing in stationary position with hands clasped and extended forward; second child moving around him in circle, stepping on each beat (minutes). When he returns to beginning position, first child moves arms clockwise to next "hour."

    b. Two children standing face to face, with arms joined at sides. One child turns outward and inward alternately (minutes) and returns to face partner on the "hour."

    c. One child turns slowly, with both arms extended sideward. Partner, with torso bent forward at waist, turns under revolving arms of first child (minutes).

    d. Partners facing with arms extended forward holding hands; knees flex and lift together on minutes; arms swing sideward on hours.

    e. Partners facing, both hands at 12 o'clock. Right hand of one partner moves from 12 to 6 o'clock; six beats in downward motion. Partner continues with other arm from 6 to 12 o'clock; six beats in upward motion. Both use percussive movements (hours).

    f. Standing one behind the other. Front child, with legs in wide stride, swings arms back and forth between legs like a pendulum (hour). Partner circles both hands above head at faster tempo (minutes).

ADDITIONAL ELEMENTS   *Use of body parts in different rhythmic patterns; spatial relationships.*

Problem III: To explore, using imagery, underlying and divided beats.

A. *In a cuckoo clock, when does the cuckoo jump out? (Children's responses: Every hour, every fifteen minutes.)*

    1. Take a partner. One person move to the steady beat of the clock; one person move only on the cuckoo.

    2. Make your own sounds on the cuckoo's beat. Feel the beat as you move together. (After movements have been improvised, accompaniment may be used only for the cuckoo or to reinforce the accented and underlying beat.)

III.A.2a *Cuckoo clock* (1)

SOLUTIONS

    a. One child arches back in bridge shape, with hands and feet on floor and stomach facing upward. "Cuckoo," on hands and knees, pops through space under arched back on the "hour."

    b. One child standing with legs together; other child crouching behind him on knees. On "cuckoo," legs open wide and "cuckoo" darts forward between them.

    c. Partners standing one in back of other. On "cuckoo," front child flexes knees in crouching position. "Cuckoo" bends forward from waist on beat.

ADDITIONAL ELEMENTS *Spatial relationships; body shape; range; difference in energy expended in the two rhythms.*

3. Work in groups of threes. Two of you move to the ticking of the clock. One person moves only on the "cuckoo." Keep the rhythm going. (Teacher picks up underlying beat on drum for each group; plays accented beat with a higher pitched instrument, for example, tone block. Children may also accompany each other.)

III.A2a *Cuckoo clock* (2)

SOLUTIONS
   a. Two children facing with arms extended sideward hold-
      ing hands, swinging back and forth. "Cuckoo" crouches
      between them. As "cuckoo" jumps up, they lower their
      bodies to a crouching position.
   b. Three children holding hands in a triangular shape, beat-
      ing time by pulling arms back and forth. "Cuckoo" ducks
      under arms of other two partners alternately (similar to
      a folk dance pattern).
   c. Two children facing, holding each other's elbows.
      "Cuckoo" crouches between them. As "cuckoo" jumps
      up, arms of partners swing open sideward.

ADDITIONAL ELEMENTS *Differences in body shape; range; level;
direction; new spatial relationships created by three people.*

B. *Machines have different rhythms and sounds; let's explore some
   of them.*

   1. Work in partners. One of you start the rhythm of a ma-
      chine part and make a sound as you move so that we can
      hear the beat.

2. The other person should find a different movement with a different rhythm and attach himself to the moving part.
3. Keep the rhythm going so that we can see which part is establishing the steady beat and which part is dividing the beats. You can be in one place or you can move through space.

SOLUTIONS
a. *Washing machine.* Partners face each other, with arms curved forward and fingers touching. One child twists torso back and forth slowly; other child twists torso side to side, making swishing sounds.
b. *Pistons.* Partners facing each other. As one child lowers torso to crouching position, with knees turned outward, other partner rises in alternating movements, both making hissing sounds.
c. *Gears.* One partner turning clockwise, with left arm extended; other child turning counterclockwise, with left arm extended. As arms meet, the impulse propels them in opposite directions, making clicking sounds.
d. *Stapler.* Partners standing back to front. Front partner walking forward and back, making clicking sounds, raising arms with flexed elbows on forward movement, lowering them to waist level on backward movements. As front child backs up, rear partner reaches around and clasps front child's hands, squeezes, and releases.

4. Both partners in the "pistons" and the "gears" are moving in the same rhythm. Trying to find two different rhythms.

SOLUTIONS
a. *Pistons.* First partner raising and lowering torso, as before, in a steady, slow tempo. Other partner crouching and lifting in half time.
b. *Gears.* One partner turning slowly clockwise with arm extended; other child standing still, with arms extended. First partner swings around, pushes arm of other child (in cam action), twirling him around.

5. Now choose as many people as you need for your machine.

SOLUTION
Typewriter (group of seven). Five children standing side by side in line as "keys." Two children as "carriage" stand facing each other perpendicular to "keys," at beginning of line, with

arms extended from shoulders, grasping forearms. As "carriage" passes, each "key" crouches, with knees completely flexed in percussive movement (as if being pushed down). At end of line, one child of "carriage" shakes body and makes ringing sound. "Carriage" then returns to beginning of line and repeats movement.

UNDERSTANDINGS FOR TEACHERS—PROBLEMS II–III

Through these explorations children become aware that rhythm is experienced as different groupings of beats. In rhythmic time the underlying pulse is established by the child, and divided beats must be sensed within his framework.

A clock is a familiar image and is easily adapted to a child's ability to establish his own "time." Working in partners gives children an opportunity to observe the relationship between different rhythms and to explore different possibilities with different body parts.

The association of sound and rhythm offers two sources for developing a "listening ear": (1) recognizing different tone qualities and rhythmic patterns made by various instruments playing together and (2) relating sounds to the movements of others.

In experiences with clocks and machines, children are combining an auditory (hearing) and kinesthetic (muscle) sense, which helps them understand that both sounds and movement form rhythmic patterns.

Problem IV: To explore the relationship between tempo and force.

A. *When you move fast or slow, you use different amounts of energy. Let's explore the feeling of heavy and slow.*

　1. Think of the biggest bell you've ever seen. Pull that big, heavy bell using your whole body. Feel the weight as you pull the rope.

　SOLUTIONS
　　a. Body plane is frontal, with arms together above head, pulling from high to low in front of body.
　　b. Body plane is diagonal, with feet in wide stride, pulling in diagonal direction across body to floor.
　　c. Body plane is frontal, with legs in sideward stride, arms

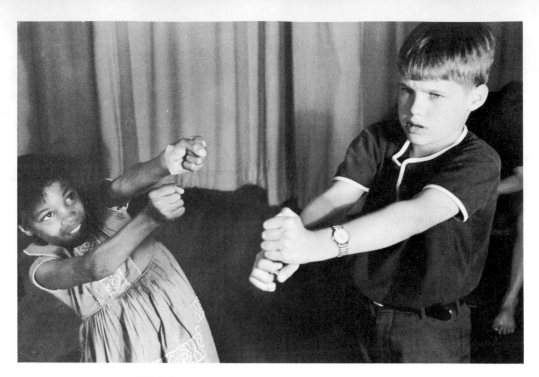

IV.A.1

extended over head, pulling in curved direction from above head through legs.

d. Body plane is frontal, with legs in wide forward stride, pulling from over head. Torso curves forward and downward to floor; head is at knee level.

ADDITIONAL ELEMENTS Force: *slow, sustained movement*; space: *range between legs, between arms and torso*; body shape; time: *rhythmic pattern of even beats*.

2. How many beats did it take each of you to ring the bell? Do it again and feel the number of beats you use to move from high to low. (Teacher may accompany on drum or gong to make children more conscious of their own rhythm.)

B. *Now let's explore the difference between* light *and* fast. *What makes a small bell ring? (Children's response: Clapper.)*

1. Work in twos. One of you move as the bell, one as the clapper.
2. Are you both moving at the same time? What is the difference in your rhythm?
3. Does the bell use the same kind of energy as the clapper when they move?

SOLUTIONS

Children who are "bells" create different body shapes of a bell (for example, torso in crouching position, with knees turned out and arms extended to sides and curved downward; torso curved forward, head downward, arms close to ears and curved around head; both shapes swinging in slow, sustained, movement). "Clappers" use different body parts (for example, one leg hitting against the other leg; head shaking, swaying, nodding; arms in striking, percussive movements).

4. Now put your movements together and each couple make a bell.

SOLUTIONS

Children establish a 3/4 rhythm to accommodate to the swinging, swaying, rocking movement of the bell. With further elaboration, bells may move in 6/8 time, clappers in 3/4; unlike the "cuckoo," which moves on the accented beat, the "clappers" move on a continuous, even beat.

5. Using machines again, make the parts move first loud and fast; then change the movements so that they are light and slow.

SOLUTIONS

In addition to vocal sounds, dynamics or force are produced by stamping feet, pounding hands on the floor, slapping different parts of the body, or taking a wider step. Slow movements tend to produce softer sounds; fast movements produce louder, percussive sounds.

UNDERSTANDINGS FOR TEACHERS—PROBLEM IV

Although the focus is on time and force, all the elements of movement are involved. As in the problem of the clocks, there are spatial relationships involving: range (space between the legs, between the arms, between the arms and torso); direction (up and down, side to side, in and out); body shape (relation of bell to clapper); rhythmic groupings (bell establishes underlying beat, clapper divides the beat). Distribution of body weight differs between slow and heavy (sustained movement) and light and fast (percussive movement).

By combining these qualities children are able to experience contrasts in the dynamics of both force and time.

Explorations in Metric Pattern

Problem I: To explore groupings of beats within a metric structure.

A. *In certain rhythms everyone moves in the same amount of time.*

    1. Jump to the beat of the drum. When the drum stops, you stop. (Teacher beats a given number of measures, using different groupings of beats, for example, 4, 5, 6, 8, 9.)

    2. How many beats did you jump? (Initially, children's responses may differ because of lack of kinesthetic awareness of movement and timing.)

    3. Listen again and jump one measure with the drum. When the drum stops, you jump the same number of beats alone. (Teacher establishes a steady beat in an even or uneven pattern.)

    4. How many beats did you jump by yourselves?

    5. Now let's take turns with the drum. Beat a measure of as many beats as you wish but keep them steady. Everyone else jump to the beat.

    6. *(To the group)* How many beats did you jump? *(To the drummer)* How many beats did you play?

B. *You can use the same number of beats but change the feeling of your movement.*

    1. How many ways can you jump? How high? How low? Can you jump forward? Backward?

    2. Jump as high as you can. What will help you jump higher? (Teacher accompanies as before.)

SOLUTIONS
Greater pushing action of the feet for elevation; knees slightly flexed; knees flexed, with heels almost touching buttocks on each jump; wider range of arms: arms stretching on the diagonal or reaching above head on each jump.

    3. Now jump high for the first measure, low on the next, medium on the next. How many measures did you jump?

    4. This time walk the first measure with the drum; on the next measure change your level and walk without the drum. When the drum begins again, rest on that measure. How many measures did you walk?

I.B *How many ways can you jump to the drum?*

C. *Different members of your family move in different ways.*

1. How do fathers walk? Everyone take space on the floor and let's hear the sound of your feet as well as see them. (After observing, teacher establishes 4/4 tempo on the drum, plays half-note value for each step.)

   SOLUTIONS
   Stamping with knees flexed; stepping with heavy tread; stamping with feet turned outward; lunging in forward strides.

2. How do mothers or grandmothers walk? How do they walk if they are wearing high heels? (Teacher plays quarter notes which are twice as fast as fathers' rhythm, using tone gourd, tone block, or tambourine.)

   SOLUTIONS
   Walking with heels slightly elevated; walking on tiptoes; walking in normal position.

3. How do babies walk? (Teacher plays eighth notes or triplets on triangle, bells, claves.)

   SOLUTIONS
   Running with short, sliding steps; running on tiptoes; running lightly; stepping alternately from side to side (waddling).

4. Divide into three groups—fathers, mothers, babies—and sit in different parts of the room; move only when you hear your rhythm; sit down quickly when another group moves. (Teacher alternates among the three groups, playing four measures of 4/4 time for each.)
5. This time you'll all move together, so listen carefully for your own rhythm and come in on beat; move in different directions and watch the space around you.
6. Let's have five or six people playing instruments—one for the fathers, two or three for mothers and grandmothers, and two or three for babies; let's have the drum set the steady tempo.
7. Now divide into smaller groups; a few of you from each group come out on the floor and establish your own rhythm; when the people with instruments feel your beat, they'll pick it up. (Alternate movers and players; smaller groups make it easier for children to observe relationship between rhythm and sound.)

Although children are responding to measurable, counted time, in the process of moving they are sensing the number of beats kinesthetically, without mechanically counting them. They are asked to count them verbally only after they have experienced them rhythmically.

For younger children the teacher controls the groupings of beats so that there is no confusion among the children as to the pattern being presented. Older children, when given time to experiment with instruments, can more readily establish a steady, consistent beat.

The association of sound *and* rhythm *again strengthens a "listening ear" and a consciousness of the relationship of both elements to movement. In part C, a "listening ear" is required of both movers and players, because they are actively involved in all three elements.*

Problem II: To explore how groupings of beats form measures.

A. *Let's put different groupings of beats together to make measures.*

1. Listen to the rhythm of the drum. If it walks, you walk. If it skips, you skip. When it stops, you stop. (Teacher beats 4/4 time—four walks, four skips, alternating for eight measures.)
2. How many times did you change from walks to skips? Now walk with the drum. Each time you hear a loud beat, move in a different direction. (Teacher plays four measures of eight beats, accents first beat of every measure.)
3. You can move in directions other than forward. Change very sharply and watch for people around you; stay on your own path.
4. How many beats did you walk before you changed directions? So how many beats are there in your measure?
5. Divide into small groups and move across the floor on the diagonal. Follow the beat of the drum, then come back the same way without the drum. (Teacher varies number of beats, rhythm, and tempo for each group.)
6. *(To the participants)* How many beats did you feel? *(To the observers)* Did they come back in as many beats as the drum played?

9. *Explorations* **153**

ADDITIONAL ELEMENTS *Spatial awareness of other moving bodies; direction, path; use of different locomotor movements relating to different rhythmic patterns played on drum.*

B. *Now you can make measures of four beats and each one of you will move on your own beat.*

1. Divide in groups of four in different parts of the room. Each person in the group count aloud so we can see how many 1's, 2's, 3's, 4's will be moving together.

2. When you hear your number, make a lunging movement into space using your whole body and hold it for all four beats. Then quickly stand up at the end of the measure and start again on 1.

3. Make a group shape as you come in "on beat." Don't touch each other, but work in the same space. (Each group may move for four measures of four beats to establish feeling of continuity. Each child's movement will differ in duration, depending on the number of his beat, for example, 1 is the longest, 4 is the shortest.)

SOLUTIONS

a. *First beat.* Torso extending forward on low level, with one leg flexed at knee in forward position, weight on ball of foot, other leg extending backward on ball of foot, both arms extended forward with hands on floor.

Second beat. Torso curving forward from waist, facing downward; weight on front leg, with knee flexed; other leg flexed and extending backward, with foot elevated from floor; both hands on floor; face down.

Third beat. Torso curving forward, with flat back; head forward; legs in wide forward stride; front leg with flexed knee; back leg straight; arms extending from shoulders in diagonal direction.

Fourth beat. Torso curving forward, with flat back, leaning over front flexed knee, head facing down, back leg extended in air, hands wide apart on floor (all facing same direction).

b. *First beat.* Standing, with feet in wide stride; torso twisting on diagonal plane downward toward left arm, which is extended downward; head curving sideward, toward arm; right arm extending diagonally and upward.

Second beat. Standing, with feet in frontward stride; back leg resting on ball of foot; torso twisting left, with arm

II.B.3a

II.B.3b

extending toward first beat; right arm extending backward.

Third beat. Standing in sideward stride, with torso twisting toward right arm, which is extended backward; left
arm down and slightly forward; head erect.

Fourth beat. Facing first beat diagonally, with torso twisting left, left arm extended and flexed inward at elbow,
head facing left shoulder, right arm extending backward.

ADDITIONAL ELEMENTS   Space: *range, level, body shape, group
shape*; force: *that required to hold duration of beat.*

UNDERSTANDINGS FOR TEACHERS—PROBLEM II

*In part A, changing the rhythm at each measure helps children
sense the length of the measure and helps them recognize and
respond quickly to different rhythmic groupings. Initially, children
may not change directions sharply, but it is part of learning to
respond to their own impulse.*

*Percussive accompaniment while children are moving reinforces
the feeling that groupings of beats fall naturally into measures;
as a result, children are better able to rely on their own kinesthetic
sense to repeat the same rhythmic patterns accurately.*

*Singing games are effective in helping very young children de-
velop a sense of measure. An example is, "Did you ever see a
Lassie?" Children alternate standing in the middle of a circle and
initiate a movement in 3/4 time to correspond to the words*

go / this way and / that way and /
3   1   2   3   1   2   3

Other examples are such songs as "Shoo, Fly, Don't Bother Me" [6]
(2/4 time) and "On, Roll On," [7] *(6/8).*

Problem III: To explore the relationship of accented beats
to time and force in movement.

A. *How can you make some movements feel more important than
others?*

   1. Listen to the beats of the drum. They may not all be the
      same, so listen first so that your body will know what to

---

[6] See *Songs to Grow On*, p. 108, listed in Bibliography.   [7] Ibid., p. 74.

do. Now jump! (Teacher first plays six beats; then eight, six even and two accented.)

2. What happens on the smaller jumps (accented beats)? What happens to your jumps when you have a longer count?

ADDITIONAL ELEMENTS Space: *on a longer beat, movement covers more space and has greater range;* force: *difference in energy expended on long and short beats.*

3. Now take an easy walk with the drum and stop when the drum stops. (Teacher beats a steady rhythm of twelve beats in 6/8 time.)
4. This time when you hear a louder beat, make a different kind of movement; put more energy into it. (Teacher plays three measures of 6/8 time, accenting first and fourth beats.)

SOLUTIONS
Children demonstrate accents by taking longer steps, taking higher steps, flexing knees and lowering torso, and clapping.

5. What other parts of your body can you use?

SOLUTIONS
Head swings from side to side and nods on accented beat; body tilts from side to side on accents; arms extend sharply sideward; arms are raised over head.

B. *Let's put some of your ideas together and combine accented and even movements.*

1. Listen to the rhythm; make a big movement on the first important beat and a smaller movement on the second accent; let your arms also move in a big and small way so that your whole body moves to the rhythm.

SOLUTIONS
(Tempo is 6/8; first accented beat is stronger than fourth accent.)

Children experience a listing, swinging movement around the accents. (Teacher may play tambourine, striking on accents and shaking on other beats.)

2. This time the rhythm is going to change; begin with the drum but listen as you are moving so you can feel the num-

ber of beats between each accent. (Teacher plays four measures of 4/4 time; accents first beat of measure.)

3. As you are walking, clap on the first beat, hop on the second, leap on the third, and jump on the fourth; walk in a big circle around the room.

4. Are you hopping and leaping on the same foot? Let's do it again.

5. Now the accented beat is going to change in each measure. Find ways of showing it in different kinds of movement. It can be louder, softer, lighter, heavier, larger, or smaller. (Teacher plays eight measures of 4/4 time and shifts accent to first, second, third, fourth beat in each succeeding measure; then she repeats the phrase:

4/4 / ———— / ———— / ———— / .
         ´   ´   ´
———— / ———— /
  ´   ´   (repeat)

ADDITIONAL ELEMENTS Space: *differentiated use of body parts (arms, head, torso, legs, feet); range; direction; level; force: contrast between more and less energy expended on accented and unaccented beats.*

UNDERSTANDINGS FOR TEACHERS—PROBLEM III

In this problem three types of responses to accented beats are experienced: an accent in relation to a grouping of beats, accents which divide beats into different rhythmic patterns (4/4, 3/4, 6/8), and irregular accents within a metric structure (of 4/4 time).

Accent, as a time–force phenomenon is expressed through different qualities of movement (light, heavy, loud, soft, large, small) and is important for further improvisations.

Problem IV: To explore phrasing in response to percussive and melodic accompaniment.

A. *Let's put measures of beats together into longer phrases.*

1. Divide into groups of four sitting in different parts of the room. (Teacher places four instruments in the middle of the floor, for example, a tone block, a maraca, claves, and a triangle.)

2. Count off as you did before so that you know who are the

1's, 2's, 3's, and 4's who will be moving together. (Groups alternate for each problem.)

3. When you hear your number, each one from a group take four giant steps toward the center, pick up an instrument in four beats, beat three beats, replace it in one beat, and walk back in four beats.

SOLUTION

Each child is responding to four measures of four beats and is establishing a phrase. In the second measure the child must sense the rhythm by playing in the same tempo.

4. Listen to the tempo of the drum; run as fast as you can to an instrument; look at it and return to your place when you hear the drumbeat. (Teacher plays eight running beats in; eight running beats out.)

SOLUTION

Each child must relate his steps to the number of beats of the drum; the pause is sensed as the end of one phrase and the beginning of another.

5. Now run to the center without accompaniment; on the drum signal, run back in the same tempo.
6. This time walk toward the center without the drum, count the number of walks in, play your instrument for the same number of beats, and walk back the same way.
7. (To the observers) How many beats did they play? (To the participants) How many beats did you walk? Not everyone used the same amount of beats in their phrases.

SOLUTION

Each child establishes a phrase composed of three parts: a–b–a (walking–playing–walking), a form used in music as well as dance. Each child creates his own rhythmic grouping within the phrase, depending upon the number of beats he uses to move through a defined space, for example, 7, 9, 10.

UNDERSTANDINGS FOR TEACHERS—PROBLEM IV

Children become aware of phrasing as groupings of measures which do not necessarily have the same number of beats and which have different patterns.

By first responding to a given pattern of measures and then repeating it by sensing the groupings of beats kinesthetically, chil-

dren are learning to demonstrate a combination of related movements that correspond to a musical phrase.

Problem V: To respond to metric patterns derived from the music and rhythm of folk songs.

A. *Let's sing this song and move to the rhythm of the words. "Clap Your Hands," American Folk Songs for Children, p. 86. (Teacher accompanies with piano, autoharp, guitar, or voice.)*

1. Sit together on the floor. While we're singing, the words will tell you what to do.

> Clap, clap, clap your hands
> Clap your hands together
> Clap, clap, clap your hands
> Clap your hands together.

(Teacher begins with body movements while children are sitting on the floor. She changes to locomotor movements within the song to move children easily out on the floor.)

> Shake, shake, shake your hands, etc. (Body movements.)
> Nod, nod, nod your head, etc.
> Twist, twist, twist yourself, etc.
> Tap, tap, tap your toes, etc.
> Swing, swing, swing your arms, etc.

2. Now let those swings take you around the room; sing it again and see if you are swinging in the same tempo as you did when you were sitting down.

> Walk, walk, walk around, etc.   (Locomotor movements.)
> Slide, slide, slide around, etc.
> Gallop, gallop, gallop around, etc.
> Walk, walk, walk around, ⎱ (Suggested by author to
> Come back and sit down. ⎰ round off phrase and bring group together.)

3. Even though the steady beat is the same, can you feel the difference between a skip, a slide, a gallop, and a swing?
4. Do them again while you're singing so that you can feel the rhythm in your muscles. You may also clap so you can hear it. (Teacher may use drum to emphasize accented beats.)

SOLUTIONS

Clapping or singing the action words helps children sense that skipping, sliding, galloping have the same accented beat and a swing has no accented beat. Rhythmic patterns of different locomotor movements are experienced as part of a general feeling for phrasing.

B. *Songs have both a steady beat and a melody. Feel the difference in these two rhythms by singing and clapping.*

1. Listen to this song; sing it with me all the way through. "Going to Boston," *Songs to Grow On*, pp. 78–79 (4/4 time).

> Come along, girls (boys), we're going to Boston
> Early in the morning   (Repeat three times.)
> *Chorus:*
> Don't we look pretty when we're dancing (skipping,
> turning, etc.)   (Repeat three times.)
> Early in the morning.

2. Sing it again and clap just the steady beat. How many beats to a measure?
3. Now just clap the melody. What do you clap in a song when you clap the melody? (Children's responses: The music, the notes, the words.) Do all the beats take the same amount of time?
4. Let's have just the girls skip to Boston first. When we sing, "Don't we look pretty when we're . . ." do any kind of movement you wish but bring it to an end on "Early in the morning," because that's the end of the phrase.
5. Now let's have the boys go to Boston; you go in a different way and make your own movements when you get there.
6. While the boys are there, the girls skip in, singing, "Come on, girls, and let's go find them . . . early in the morning." When you're all in Boston, take a partner and move together.

C. *In this song it's the music and the rhythm that will give you ideas for movements, not the words. "Up on the Mountain," Songs to Grow On, p. 110 (4/4 time).*

> Up on the mountain, two by two   (Repeat three times.)
> Rise, sugar, rise.
> *Chorus:*
> Let me see you make a motion,
> two by two   (Repeat three times.)
> Rise, sugar, rise.

That's a very poor motion,
    indeed it is   (Repeat three times.)
Rise, sugar, rise.
Let me see you make another
    one, two by two   (Repeat three times.)
Rise, sugar, rise.
That's a very fine motion,
    indeed it is   (Repeat three times.)
Rise, sugar, rise.
Down from the mountain, two
    by two   (Added by author.)
Shine, sugar, shine.

1. Do you know what a motion is? (Children's responses: Wriggle or make gestures to show movement.)
2. Work "two by two." Take your partner's hand and walk "up on the mountain" around in a big circle; on "rise, sugar, rise" drop hands and face your partner so everyone is standing in an inside and outside circle (in two lines). (If group is too large, half may dance while the others sit and sing.)
3. Find a movement that you can do together using your whole body; explore moving in different directions and on different levels.
4. What are your feet doing? Your arms? Do your feet have their own rhythm? Do your arms have a different rhythm?

SOLUTIONS
First couple. Jumping up and down on both feet, turning in opposite directions, using eight beats to complete turn.
Second couple. Stepping sideward in wide stride for two beats, shifting weight to alternate feet, swinging arms parallel to legs.
Third couple. Holding hands, beginning with arms extended sideward, swinging them to center over head (between partners); balancing forward together on one foot, then stepping back to other foot as arms move sideward.
Fourth couple. Holding hands, standing shoulder to shoulder, sliding four steps to right, four steps to left.

5. (After "That's a pretty motion. . . .") Some people are moving with their whole bodies, some just with their legs or arms; develop a full body motion together.

SOLUTIONS
Fifth couple. Arms moving together in swinging movement from side to center; jumping high, with legs in wide sideward stride, one jump for each beat.

Sixth couple. Arms extending forward; holding hands, partners moving up and down in opposition, bending knees, crouching, and rising. Each motion lasts for two beats.

Seventh couple. In backward and forward direction, one partner stepping forward on one leg extending arms from shoulders for two beats, shifting weight to back leg as arms open sideward for two beats. Partner moving in reverse direction (one forward, one back).

ADDITIONAL ELEMENTS Space: *exploration of fuller body movement leads to greater use of space, for example, range, direction (back and forth, up and down, diagonal), level; force: expressed through accented beats.*

UNDERSTANDINGS FOR TEACHERS—PROBLEM V

In this problem metrical rhythm is defined in musical form. Children initially respond to folk songs in different ways. Some are stimulated by the melodic qualities so that the primary impression is auditory; some sense the underlying or accented beats so that they respond rhythmically; others listen only for the words and use them as movement cues.

The advantage of folk songs for young children is that in addition to being charming and easy to learn, they call forth more than one sensory impression. For example, a song such as "Up on the Mountain" has an attractive melody, simple and repetitive words, and an adaptable rhythm; it merely asks children to "make a motion," without further instruction. (There are many folk songs that are also effective with older children.)

In this song moving to phrasing in partners requires that children adapt to a unified rhythmic pattern while picking up movement cues from each other. Each couple should be encouraged to develop their own pattern "two by two," with the stated expectation that every couple will find its own form of expression. (See Part VI, "Resources," for collections of folk songs.)

Accompaniment and Sound

For children, an awareness of time patterns is reinforced and heightened by the use of musical or percussive accompaniment. For teachers, whether they play the piano, guitar, or autoharp, instruments offer a rich source for rhythmic experiences.

A collection of instruments for the classroom should include as many variations as possible. Along with the excitement of having them available, children must also recognize that they are not noise-making objects to be "played with," but to be "played." As such, they are a part of the necessary and valuable equipment of learning. While they should be relatively inexpensive, they should also be as close to professional tone quality as possible. (Homemade instruments serve a different purpose, and although it is interesting for children to see how combinations of materials produce sounds, this is not the concern here.)

Of all the musical instruments which have evolved through time, the simplest and closest to movement are the *percussion instruments*. Although all instruments that we strike or beat are called percussive, each has its unique tone and texture. As a way of noting similarities and differences between them, we might suggest that children think in terms of "families" of sound and the types of movements which produce them. Instruments may, for example, be divided into four families:

1. Beating and pounding, which produces deep, resonant sounds (of short or long duration).

    drums or gongs

2. Shaking, which produces higher tones with delicate or heavy textures (of short duration).

    tambourines (to beat as well as shake)
    wrist bells
    ankle bells
    maracas
    Indian rattles (gourds)
    African seed pod rattles

3. Shaking or hitting, which produces sharp, clear sounds ranging from high to middle tones (of short duration).

    finger cymbals
    hand cymbals
    triangles
    claves
    castenets
    tone blocks
    bamboo sticks
    Chinese temple blocks
    xylophone

164

4. Scraping and rubbing, which produces scratching or rough textures (long or short duration).

   tone gourd
   raspa
   sand blocks

With the exception of large drums, gongs, xylophones, and Chinese temple blocks (when attached to a stand), all the instruments listed are easily handled and can be played while moving. This is not to suggest that instruments should always be played while children are moving or that the same children should necessarily do both. It is merely to point out that they are convenient for young children because they can either be held or worn on the body. The choice of instruments, the way they are used and by whom, must grow out of the nature of the rhythmic problem to be explored.

There are dynamic qualities in every movement pattern which must be sensed if the accompaniment is to reflect and accentuate these qualities. As children freely explore an instrument to get a tangible feeling of its size, shape, weight, and the different ways it can be played, they become aware that there is a relationship between sound and movement in each tonal "family." In so doing, they

experience the idea that the energy which produces a sound can also be felt in the body.

For example, a long, sustained movement which brings forth vibrations from a gong may be expressed as a smooth, continuous swing, in contrast to the short vibrations produced by striking a triangle. Shaking bells or maracas may stimulate vibratory movements. The difference between shaking and beating a tambourine may reflect differences in percussive movements. Claves or tone blocks may elicit short, sharp, staccato movements. And the xylophone, which most closely resembles the piano, may range from stretching or sustained movement relating to the broad sweep of the keyboard, to separate impulses comparable to individual notes.

If faced with the choice of buying only one instrument for the classroom, a teacher might well select a drum as being the most versatile. It has the widest range of intensity and can accompany movements which are loud at one moment and barely audible in the next. Also, simple beats are more keenly heard and sensed kinesthetically than melody or harmony and therefore may evoke more direct movement responses. Because of these features it is perhaps the most important of the percussion instruments.

For teachers new to dance, it may be instructive first to observe children walk or skip normally around the room, and pick up their tempo on the drum. This gives some insight as to the general tempo level of the age group with which a teacher is involved. It also permits her to note individual differences among children's movements, even when they accommodate to each other with the same walking beat.

The drum serves to sharpen children's perception of both metric and rhythmic time. If, for example, a teacher's intent is to encourage an awareness of metrical groupings in measures and phrases, she may establish the pattern in a simple problem such as, "Step each time you hear a beat; when I stop, you stop; when I begin, you move again in a different direction." In this way children can feel the number of beats in a measure and recognize how many measures of movements have formed a phrase.

Similarly, children may be asked to make a movement which corresponds to the underlying beat, as established by the teacher, and then to move a different way to the accented or unaccented beats. Although the steady beat is provided, the intervening movements that they design will help to clarify the relationship. Children can demonstrate ways in which metric time is divided (for example, by using different parts of their bodies to express duration). For example, a whole note of four beats may be a sustained movement of the torso, half notes may be shown by a movement of the arms, and quarter notes may be shown by movements of the legs. Although the style or quality of movements may vary with each child, they are responding to a basic rhythmic pattern defined by the drum. With this approach it becomes apparent that a teacher's sense of rhythm must be fairly accurate and that she must develop facility in using the drum. A small drum held in the hand is preferable, for it allows her to move freely among the children if she feels the need to do so.

When the teacher's intent is to help children strengthen their own rhythmic patterns, the drum serves to accompany rather than lead. If, for example, children are exploring different qualities of rhythm using machines as imagery, the form each child creates will have its own internal rhythm, whether or not he is aware of it at the moment. In this case, the drum may clarify or intensify a rhythmic pattern. In contrast to metric accompaniment, where movements must be directly related to sounds, the purpose here is to define and reinforce movements within the structure a child sets for himself.

In this type of accompaniment, a teacher's feeling for tempo is probably the most critical element, because each individual or group has a unique tempo which gives organization to the movement. It is essential that the drum "pick up" the underlying pulse established by the children, for if such accompaniment is not minimally supportive, they find it difficult to continue the movement and general confusion may ensue. Just as a child needs time to coordinate rhythmic elements, so a teacher needs to observe how those elements work together. A more effective relationship between sound and movement may be achieved if children are encouraged to experiment before any tempo is set.

It is perhaps important to note, at this point, that although the drum (or any other percussive instrument) has an important function, it does not necessarily ensure the successful execution of a movement. There are instances in which children can best express themselves in an atmosphere of silence, relying on the body alone to project a sense of time.

The decision as to when and how frequently to use the drum or other instruments may first rest with the teacher, but

167

children must be helped to develop this sensitivity when they accompany each other. Initially, instruments may be made available in two ways: (1) they may be given out randomly, without regard for children's preferences, because lack of experience gives them little basis for selective judgments; or (2) each child's preference may be met with the clear understanding that all instruments will be shared, especially the drum, which is the most frequently sought after. In either case, a successful introduction of instruments usually depends on a teacher's perception of the listening and responding abilities of her group and on how comfortable she feels in a situation which may have a rather cacophonous and noisy beginning.

Because instruments are valued as sound-producing materials, in presenting them to children, teachers should have certain criteria in mind: (1) that their tone quality be pleasing and stimulating; (2) that they are easy to manipulate; (3) that they vary in timbre, pitch, duration, and volume; and (4) that they complement creative experimentation in dance by offering a wide range of sounds and tones.

Although we are concerned primarily with dance and not with the technical aspects of sound, the latter has special characteristics which can be made comprehensible to young children. *Timbre* is the distinctive resonance resulting from the particular material or shape of an instrument (for example, a small drum and a tone block may have the same pitch but their resonance is different). *Pitch* is the "highness" or "lowness" of a musical tone, which depends on the number of vibrations per second and the resultant number of sound waves per second which reach the ear (for example, when a string is plucked, the number of vibrations is great, so that the pitch is high; a large drum as contrasted with a small one produces fewer vibrations, so the sound is lower). *Volume* is the degree of loudness or intensity of a sound. *Duration* is that portion of time given to a sound or tone.

Just as dance is the shaping of the body, so instruments are the shaping of sound, and each contributes its own aesthetic qualities to the total experience. In a flexible situation, the dynamic qualities of sound can act as an impetus for movement, just as dynamic qualities of movement can provide exciting patterns for sounds. In order for children to become conscious of this relationship, we suggest that they need to develop a "listening ear." In a metaphoric sense, the image is of a sharpened rhythmic and musical perception based on a child's growing ability to become aware of contrasts and to respond to change. Listening, feeling, and responding become part of the process of kinesthetic awareness and are necessary in achieving self-control.

It is as important for a teacher to help a child develop a "listening ear" in relation to his own accompaniment as it is with those who are moving to it. Whether he initiates a new pattern or incorporates someone else's, he must sense its qualities with the same intensity as those who are responding to the rhythm they hear. The same holds when children are simply experimenting with instruments in small groups apart from movement. They usually display great interest in playing ensemble and can learn much from observing and listening to each other.

If instruments are a new experience, however, children tend to play separately from each other, even when accompanying movement. When given time to explore each instrument in terms of the characteristics described, they can begin to make judgments as to which instruments might be most appropriate for particular movement problems and which would be most effective in combinations. As they gain experience in playing to-

gether, group improvisations may emerge which complement improvisations in movement. Frequently it is the teacher who must make children aware of their own creative efforts in this regard, just as interesting movements need to be called to their attention.

We may also anticipate that a new exposure to instruments may produce quite different results. It is what usually occurs when children simply pick up an instrument and "play" with no understanding of its qualities or of the problem to which it is related. Waterman, writing in 1937, observed that, "The selection of the particular instruments used should be given thought. Poor tonal quality in the instruments and disregard for their differences of timbre, can destroy a child's sensitivity toward sound." [8] She goes on to comment on a situation which unfortunately still prevails in most classrooms where instruments are provided. "Banging every instrument on every beat is characteristic of some kindergarten or rhythm bands. Not even in the kindergarten is this necessary, and certainly not in the elementary grades." [9]

[8] Elizabeth Waterman, *The Rhythm Book* (New York: A. S. Barnes & Co., 1937), p. 68.
[9] Ibid.

The approach presented here supports the idea that children, even in kindergarten, can be selective and discriminating in their use of instruments. In some of the dance problems included in this section, specific instruments are suggested as a way of introducing fundamental rhythmic responses. In others, the selection is left to the teacher and/or the child.

The type of grouping suggested in an earlier chapter may be interpreted here as a fluid division of "players" and "performers." As we are not concerned with rhythm band as such, it is not necessary for everyone to play at once, or to play all the time. Children should be divided so that some accompany while others dance, if not in one session, in another. Even if a group is playing ensemble, not all of the sounds may be suitable at the same time. Rather, instruments should be played according to the particular tone quality which they express in relation to the movement.

When instruments function as an integral part of the dance experience, children are given another mode of transforming rhythm through sound as well as movement. Each form has its own meaning and can exist independently, yet when put together in combinations, each

acts to intensify the other. In its most direct relationship, the dynamic values of the two run parallel; that is, the underlying pulse and beats follow a similar pattern, with comparable intensities in sounds and movements.

As a somewhat more complicated variation, tones or sounds are played in opposition, or counterpoint, as it is called in music; that is, the dynamics of the movement and that of the accompaniment may be reversed. For example, the tendency is to respond to a low pitch with low, heavy movements. However, to express a particular idea or mood, it is just as conceivable to create high, percussive movements to a low pitch, in the same way that tones leading up the scale may accompany movements which flow in a downward direction.

Apart from conventional instruments, children always have themselves as sources of sound. The *voice*, for example, is the most natural accompaniment to the body's movement and is most apt to express its internal rhythms. Exploration of breathing is an excellent way of making children aware that their voices can produce different sound qualities without becoming literal (such as "choo-choo" for a train). As a simple problem, children may be asked slowly to fill up their chest

170

cavities with air, like a balloon, and make a sound while inhaling and releasing it. In all likelihood, their "oo-ah-oh" will reflect tones in upward and downward directions. Similarly, producing tones without words may stimulate movements which are freer than those related to specific images (for example, yawning and sighing may become sustained and collapsing movements; clicking may lead to sharp, percussive movements; buzzing may be transformed into vibratory movements).

Hands and feet offer still other possibilities. Stamping and clapping introduce both an auditory and kinesthetic sensation which frequently serves to reinforce an awareness of time patterns. For example, stamping the steady beat while clapping the metrical rhythm may help children feel the relationship of one to the other. Or the same may be achieved in stamping the accents while clapping the unaccented beats. In developing rhythmic patterns a child's own sense of rhythmic groupings may be clarified if he claps while moving, so that he can both hear and feel the beat.

Different sounds made by clapping or slapping various parts of the body may be used to show contrast and change. Dynamics, as an element of sound, may reflect changes in tempo, may produce more intensity within the same tempo, or may accentuate transitions between measures and phrases.

Regardless of what medium is used to express sounds or tones, our purpose is to provide children with opportunities to develop a *"listening ear"* and to become *consciously rhythmical* by creating and responding to accompaniments which reflect the quality of movement as well as its rhythmic structure.

Finally, the instrument with the greatest scope available to the teacher is the piano. It is a rewarding attribute when teachers are able to play well enough to accompany movement. The question of whether such talent can be utilized depends upon the accessibility of a piano. Ideally, there should be one in every elementary classroom, or at least in a room that is available for dance.

The physical position of the piano vis-à-vis the children merits special thought. As considerable emphasis has been placed on rearranging the environment for dance, a piano becomes an important feature of that environment. Just as we do not teach reading to children while facing away from them, so must we devise an arrangement for movement which is comfortable for both a teacher and the children. Instead of the conventional position of the piano against a wall, which places the teacher with her back to the group, the keyboard should be sideways or perpendicular to the dance area. In this way a teacher can both face the piano and be free to turn her head to the side to observe the children.

Teachers do not have to rely on printed music. With the exception of folk songs, which have relatively simple harmonic patterns (see bibliography of music books), most music composed for dance requires considerable skill. Because one of the main virtues of the piano is that it offers rhythmic as well as melodic qualities, teachers with limited facility do not need to play in full scales or chords. Tone clusters (groups of adjacent notes played as one sound) on either white or black notes provide both percussive sounds and variations in pitch (analogous to levels in space), depending upon their direction up and down the keyboard. Interesting effects can also be produced by using only the black keys (pentatonic scales) in open melodic patterns. They offer a release from the conventional eight notes of a diatonic scale and a freer melodic form.

For teachers who can read music slightly or are acquainted with the structure of scales, basic harmonies can be developed. Most simply, a melodic line may be played in parallel intervals of thirds, sixths, or eighths (in relation to the tonic or first note of the scale). Thus, going up the C major scale, intervals of thirds would be as follows:

C–E; D–F; E–G; F–A; G–B; A–C; B–D; C–E (high).

Sixths are less symmetrical, but may be more interesting, depending upon the type of movement. Eighths are the two notes at the beginning and end of the octave which are of different pitch but of the same tone. To add more fullness, the melodic line can also be accompanied by the basic I–V chords in the base, which are built on the first and fifth notes of the scale. Thus, again in the key of C, chords are composed of the first, third, and fifth note (C, E, and G, which is a triad) or just on the first and fifth notes (C and G).

For those teachers who are conversant with music, the piano should be considered as an orchestra unto itself, for its range, textures, and dynamics give it all the qualities provided by other percussion instruments. Comparable to the drum, but with the additional facility of producing melody, accompaniment takes two approaches. One is to begin with the individual or group and to adjust to the rhythmic patterns and qualities of movement in whatever form is taking shape. In this case, a teacher must be sensitive to the changes in dynamics and moods and follow them with variations in *pitch* (high, medium, and low), *tempo* (allegro–moderato–lento), and *dynamics* (fortissimo to pianissimo), using simple chords and melodic groupings (atonal clusters, open chords, harmonic intervals).

A choice of appropriate alternatives must also be weighed against the value of no accompaniment for a period of time. Even music which emerges from within the dance experience tends to structure movement prematurely if children are not given sufficient time to work out their own improvisations. The question as to when and how to use music must be specifically related to the elements of the problem being solved.

The other is a more formal approach wherein a musical pattern is played before the children move, so that they listen and respond to whatever rhythmic groupings are being emphasized. They may be asked to move to the underlying beat or only with the accents, or to improvise movements which correspond to every note of the melody. In any case, it is important that children sense the rhythm and quality of the music before they re-

spond to it. This means that they listen to it consciously and get an over-all feeling of its time structure by allowing it to penetrate the body as well as the ears. If children are then asked to "come in on beat," they must discover the impulse by means of a repetitive movement which gives it emphasis.

Moving to music combines an auditory and kinesthetic awareness of rhythm as well as an appreciation of the function of melody. In problems of metrical rhythm designed to coordinate movement with music, children's responses should become less and less random, so that eventually they are able to begin and end "on beat," define a measure of beats, and extend movements into patterned phrases.

In either approach, music should play a recessive but "felt" role as another sensory experience in rhythmic expression. At no time, therefore, should musical accompaniment be so "heavyhanded" in quality or timbre as to overpower or displace the intent of children's movement. Even with considerable dexterity at the piano, teachers will find that composing simple harmonies to the melodic lines makes for greater clarity in helping children understand the relationship between sound and movement. The focus here is

on dance as the primary image, and the
piano and all other percussive instruments
serve only as supporting and embellishing
elements.

10. *Concept: force*

Just as the child is the center of reference in his perception of space and time, so his own body weight becomes his reference point in his understanding of other weights. He becomes aware of weight through an internal force which he creates (tension) and through an external force which acts upon his body (gravity).

Gravity is a force that constantly affects our movements, yet children are not usually conscious of its influence until they experience its whole range, from tension to relaxation. Through dance explorations they discover that some states of tension enable them to resist gravity, just as various stages of relaxation cause them to "give in" or submit to it. As a suggested vocabulary for young children, tension may be expressed as "feeling the strength in your muscles," and relaxation as "letting the energy flow out."

By exploring different qualities of force children can understand how their own body weight functions in executing movements. Variations of tension may be sensed by simple contractions and extensions of the muscles known to them as "bending and stretching." They learn too that any response to gravity carries a feeling of heaviness or lightness. For example, in exploring the difference between pushing or pulling, children become aware that in order to "keep their balance," they must control their energy from the center of the body. In contrast, circular movements such as turning or twirling bring a sensation of lightness or weightlessness. Jumping or leaping are resisting gravity while falling; collapsing is acquiescing completely.

As a concept, movement is affected by force in the following ways: (1) by the external forces of gravity and momentum, (2) by the control and flow of energy applied to the muscles, and (3) by the tempo of a movement against a resistant force (real or imagined).

As an expressive element, force as tension is created by degrees of resistance in the body and is sensed kinesthetically as *muscle tension*. A child can increase the feeling or awareness of tension in many ways. Most basic perhaps are those which heighten an awareness of his own center of gravity and his sense of balance with the transference of body weight. Although the center of gravity refers to the point from which energy is released or controlled, there is no specific "point" located in the same place on every child. It is actually an area made up of three planes—the vertical, the horizontal, and the lateral, which come together somewhere within the center of the torso.

175

A child may, however, locate his center or "middle" when he places his feet together and he is standing erect. At the same time, he can sense that as soon as he moves from an aligned position, either by moving any part of his body in space or by taking a step, there is a change in the distribution of body weight. Whether he is leaning as far as he can in one direction or is moving from a hop to a skip, he feels the change in body weight. Through experimenting with different types of movement, he soon realizes that *body weight* and *balance* are closely related. Children can sense this relationship as it appears in different time–space patterns by exploring changes in dynamics and tempo. For example, children can create movements in response to verbal similes such as "quiet as a . . .," "loud as a . . .," "heavy as a . . .," "light as a . . .," or they may respond to imagery which evokes tension states, such as pushing a heavy object across the room, pulling a heavy rope, and so on.

Force, as the third essential element of dance, is thus experienced as the amount of tension or stress of a movement. It may be defined as the flow and control of energy. Children experience qualities of force as greater or lesser tension, resistance or acquiescence to the pull of gravity,

heaviness or lightness. By varying the amount of energy in alternate ways, children become aware of different qualities of movement.

Through movement exploration, whether locomotor or axial, force comes into being through the use of *dynamics*, which are sensed as changes in the release or compression of energy. Just as there are varying divisions within time, expressed as rhythm, so do dynamics involve changes and contrasts in the output of energy familiarly known to children as heavy–light, strong–weak, fast–slow.

The qualities of force are expressed as distinct characteristics of movement which in dance terminology are called *sustained, percussive, swinging,* and *vibratory.*

Sustained movement is expressed as a smooth, constant flow of energy, such as responding to the sounds of a gong, pushing the air away from the body, or lifting an imaginary heavy object. The degree of muscle tension may be great or slight, with tempo varying according to the activity. Sustained movements are not the same as those which occur at the end of a swing or a "throw" because they are not momentary suspensions. Through the use of full body as well as body parts, children can identify this movement as having no sharp accents and no sharp beginnings and ends.

Percussive movement has the opposite feeling from sustained movement. It is a sudden, explosive release of energy in quick, sharp movements. It varies in tempo and range, and has a similar quality to the beat of a drum or triangle, or to the shake of maracas or wrist bells. If short, percussive movements quicken in tempo, they may take on a vibratory effect. The degree of force may vary, but the movement is initiated with intensity and the impetus is stopped abruptly. Since it may begin and end at any point, it lacks continuity. Children find this type of movement most comfortable because it usually corresponds to their own tempo levels.

A *swinging* movement describes the movement of a part of the body in an arc or circle around a stationary center. Children come to know this vocabulary as *axial* or *body* movement, as opposed to locomotor movement, which takes the body through space. A swing is sensed as the release of the swinging part into gravity, and it is the force of gravity and the lack of force in the muscles which initiates the action. As a swing picks up momentum, there is an acceleration which gives it impulse. The highest point of suspen-sion is like the end of a deep breath which is released slowly, giving a deceleration of energy in the final phase. Tempo varies but children soon realize that a swinging movement takes more time in its execution than a percussive movement.

Vibratory movement is a series of fluttery, staccato, back-and-forth movements, with force continually being expended and checked. In quality they are percussive movements which stop and go in quick succession. Children experience them as a sense of quivering and shaking, ranging all the way from a butterfly's wings to the mechanical vibrations of a machine.

Through various forms of problem solving using these elements within the total space–time–force framework, children come to realize that hands, feet, arms, and head are capable of moving at different speeds and with different intensity, that the torso can show both heavy and light movement in varying amounts of space and time, and that the whole body functions as an integrating and expressive medium. It is force, however, which gives quality to the action "between" movements and which helps a child maintain a sensitive balance between the parts of his body for the performance of expressive movement.

Explorations in Sustained Movement

Problem I: To experience sustained movement as tension and relaxation.

A. *Some movements we make are just like breathing—big and strong, weak and little, slow and even.*

   1. Sit together on the floor. Press your hands into your chest and take a deep breath. As you let it out, push the air away from you, slowly, slowly.

      SOLUTIONS
      (Children extend arms forward in different tempos and with varying degrees of force.)
      a. Torso is erect, pushing with elbows slightly bent and palms forward.
      b. Torso leaning forward, pushing with elbows slightly bent and hands flexed.
      c. Torso is bending forward from hips; arms extending from shoulders, with hands flexed and fingers wide apart.
      d. Body rising to knees; arms extending forward and downward, with hands flexed.

   2. Pull the air back toward you as if it were really heavy; take a breath and keep the movement slow and even.
   3. When you bring it back to your chest, explode it out in all directions; let's hear your breath "swoosh" out at the same time.
   4. Now slowly lift the air in your hands over your head and drop it down fast; scoop it up again and drop it down; let your head follow the movement.
   5. This time feel the space between your arms; scoop up as much air as you can over your head; hold it there a moment and let it flow gently down to the floor. (Repeat several times for a feeling of the continuous flow of energy.)

      ADDITIONAL ELEMENTS Time: *phrasing; contrast of fast and slow expressed through tension and relaxation;* space: *increased range of arms and torso; beginning of swinging movement.*

B. *Let's explore the feeling of "slow and heavy" using your whole body.*

   1. Stand with your feet slightly apart. You're going to fold and unfold, as if each part of you were very heavy.

I.A.1

I.A.5

2. Feel the weight from the top of your head and let it carry your body slowly downward; drop from your shoulders, your waist, your hips, until you feel folded in half.

3. Rest! Now use different parts of your body to unfold; feel that you have strings pulling you up from your behind, your back, your shoulders, your neck, and lastly, your head. [Teacher may accompany on drum to establish slow tempo and an even grouping of beats for phrasing (for example, eight beats to fold, four to rest, eight to unfold).]

4. This time, bounce with the drum so that each part of your body drops lower and lower; when your hands touch the floor, bounce up again in the same way. [Teacher plays three beats for each body part, including the rest (for example, six measures of three beats for each phrase).]

ADDITIONAL ELEMENTS Time: *responding to beat, phrasing;* space: *levels, body shape.*

Problem II: To explore qualities of force using different body parts.

A. *Feel the difference between bending and stretching in other parts of your body.*

1. Sit on the floor; open your legs as wide as you can and let your energy flow right out of your toes. (Teacher sitting on floor with children may demonstrate the difference in the stretch between flexed and pointed toes.)

2. Sit as straight as you can and push your arms out from your shoulders; feel a long stretch from the middle of your body to your fingertips.

3. Can you reach over and touch the foot on the same side as your hand? What is your other arm doing? Is your body bending or stretching?

SOLUTIONS

Sitting with legs in wide stride, one arm reaching toward foot (hand touching ankle, top of foot, or toes, depending upon extent of stretch); torso bending at waist; opposite arm extending diagonally in air, stretching that side of torso.

4. Can you touch your toes with both hands at the same time? Feel the difference in the stretch when your toes are up and when they are pointed down. Where do you feel the stretch?

II.A.1

II.A.3
Solutions

II.A.4

Stretching is sensed in the muscles of the back, arms, and thighs; greater tension is felt in the body when toes are curved downward, because more force is needed.

5. Bounce with the drum, then come back to a sitting position very slowly. (Teacher plays a given number of measures of bounces and one measure for rising.)

B. *You can also stretch the same part of your body in different ways.*

1. Have you seen a cat stretch its back? Find a position so that you can stretch just your back and feel it in your muscles. Move slowly and evenly.

SOLUTIONS
Weight on hands and knees; arms with elbows flexed; backs curved in varying degrees, with head up, forward, or down.

2. That's only one shape and you can even make that stretch feel stronger. Where do the muscles in your stomach go when you curve your back?

SOLUTIONS
a. Weight on hands and knees; arms straight; back in long curve; stomach muscles pulled in; neck flexed; head downward, following shape of back.
b. Weight distributed between knees and fingertips; arms straight; long curve from lower torso makes back high and curved; head down.

3. Change the shape smoothly from a curve to an arch. Where do you feel the change in your muscles?

SOLUTIONS
In same position on hands and knees, back arches and elongates torso; arms are slightly curved, with elbows flexed; neck flexed, with head raised, continues arched shape of back.

UNDERSTANDINGS FOR TEACHERS—PROBLEMS I–II

By exploring such natural movements as pushing, pulling, bending, and stretching, children begin to identify sustained movement as a continuous flow of impulses marked by contrast in tension and relaxation. Associating such qualities with breathing helps reinforce the organic relationship between the strength of a movement and the ability to release and control energy.

II.B.2a

Because force only exists in space–time, exerting effort in different body parts produces an awareness that each part uses a larger or smaller range of space and creates a different body shape, and that a slow, even tempo produces a special kind of rhythmic pattern.

II.B.2b

Problem III: To explore different elements of sustained movement using imagery.

A. *How many ways can you push a doorbell without using your hands?*

   1. It's a small doorbell. What parts would you use to push it?

   SOLUTIONS
   a. Standing, with one leg extending forward, "rings" bell with pointed toe.
   b. Torso leaning forward over standing leg, one leg extending backward, "rings" bell with pointed toe.
   c. Torso erect, with neck flexed and head extending forward, "rings" bell with nose.
   d. Torso bending forward from waist; one arm extending forward from shoulder; "rings" bell with flexed elbow.
   e. Torso leaning sideward; one arm is extending laterally from shoulder; "rings" bell with flexed elbow.

   2. It's a heavy doorbell. What parts of you can push it?

   SOLUTIONS
   a. Standing, kicking forward, flexing and extending knee, and pushing bell with flexed foot.
   b. Torso leaning backward, with back arched, arms extending forward, walking in wide lunging steps and pushes bell with stomach.
   c. Torso flexed at hips, with back parallel to floor, arms flexed at elbows with hands on hips, walking backward with knees turned out and pushes bell with head.
   d. Torso curved forward, head down, arms extending forward with palms down, push bell with back of wrists.
   e. Torso erect, legs in wide lateral stride, hands over head, pushes bell with one hip extending sideward.

   3. Ring your doorbell more than once with the same part of your body. Ring it in the same rhythm three times.

   ADDITIONAL ELEMENTS *Rhythm is added as another dimension of force; that is, ringing three beats is a measure; if repeated several times it becomes a phrase.*

   4. Now push a doorbell with two parts of your body, using light and heavy rings.

   SOLUTIONS
   a. *Elbow and knee.* Standing on one leg, flexing elbow and

knee of opposite arm and leg, elbow pushing with heavy ring; knee pushing with light.

b. *Legs.* Lying on back, with legs extending upward and diagonally, pushing alternately with heavy and light movements.

c. *Arms.* Sitting with feet on floor, with knees flexed and arms extending sideward, alternately pushing with palms, three heavy rings to one side, three light rings to the other.

d. *Elbow and nose.* Standing, torso bending forward from hips; back of neck flexed, with face forward; one elbow flexed; pushing with elbow and nose.

B. *Can you stretch different parts of your body just like a rubber band?*

1. Sit on the floor; imagine that you have a rubber band between your hands; stretch it as long as you can and make it small again.

2. If you pull it too fast it will snap, so move very slowly; feel the pull in your hands and bring it back the same way.

SOLUTIONS [1]

a. Sitting position. Weight resting on one side of body on one hand and one leg with foot on floor; on other side of body, arm, "pulls" toe, stretching leg upward to almost full extension. Space between is created by imaginary rubber band.

b. Lying position. Arms and leg on one side of body resting on floor; other arm curved, with flexed elbow "pulling" leg perpendicular to body.

c. Standing position. Weight is on straight leg and hand holding on to bookcase; other hand pulling toe of other leg backward and upward so that leg is in full extension.

C. *When you look in a mirror, the "other you" seems to move exactly as you do.*

1. Take a partner and face each other; one of you be the person; the other be the image in the mirror.

2. The mirror is only up to your waist, so use only the upper part of your body.

[1] Solutions to this problem may be seen in the film "Children Dance," produced and co-directed by the author and Naima Prevots. See bibliography.

III.B.2b

3. Use as much space as you wish but keep looking in the mirror, so that you are watching each other.
4. The "person" will begin the movement; keep it even in space and time so that your image will feel what you are doing and can follow.
5. After you've explored each other's movements, we will look at each couple; we should be able to tell which person is leading the movement. (Group observes and makes suggestions as to which child is initiating the movement; then children change roles.)

SOLUTIONS
Movements require isolation of upper torso and use of upper body parts (head, shoulders, arms, hands); lower torso remains still. All elements of movement are involved—*time:* establishing a tempo that partner can follow (slower tempo requires more control of energy); *spatial patterns:* range, body shape, focus; *laterality:* (right and left sidedness) response to a reversed "mirror image."

6. What qualities of movement did you use to stay together—fast, slow, big, small, light, heavy?
7. Some of you made very small gestures; feel that you are moving in slow motion because you want your image to know what you are doing.
8. Now the mirror is from your head to the floor; use full body

movement and focus on your partner all the time so that you don't lose each other.

SOLUTIONS

(Although examples are described, movements are continually changing with increased sustained quality.)

    a. *Body movements. Bending* and *stretching* from low to high, high to low, with arms moving with body as it raises and lowers; *swinging* and *swaying* from side to side, with feet stationary, swinging up and down and on the diagonal; *twisting* from side to side, looking at partner over inside shoulder; *turning* in parallel directions, focusing over each shoulder as body rotates.

    b. *Locomotor movements.* Stepping, striding, lunging forward and backward, up and down, side to side.

ADDITIONAL ELEMENTS Space: *direction, level, range, body shape, focus;* time: *coordinating tempo and rhythmic patterns.*

UNDERSTANDINGS FOR TEACHERS—PROBLEM III

Pushing a door bell and stretching a rubber band are images which are used to express simple, conventional gestures in movement terms.

In part A, for example, how does a child control his energy in different parts of his body when he changes from heavy to light movements? How does he become aware that large and small body parts can move in different rhythms which reflect the amount of force he uses? In both A and B, how does he control body weight when he is coordinating the force in two body parts?

Part C also derives from a conventional image but the response is not pantomime (that is, literal gestures such as brushing teeth, combing hair, washing face, or making faces). If such gestures are used initially, the qualities of movement need to be exaggerated and abstracted. Essentially, children are responding to each other kinesthetically, through movement cues using the basic elements of time and space as well as force.

Problem IV: To experience sustained movement in relation to balance and body weight.

A. *Feel how much energy it takes to lift one part of your body.*

    1. Sit on the floor and lift one leg very slowly as high as you can.

2. Can you keep your knee straight? What is your other leg doing?

3. How are you supporting your body?

SOLUTIONS

    a. Lying on floor with flat back, with elbows flexed and hands behind head; one leg extending while other leg rests on floor, on heel.

    b. Torso leaning backward, with weight on elbows of both arms; one leg extending while other leg rests on side of foot with flexed knee.

    c. Torso leaning slightly backward, with weight on arms extended to sides and hands on floor; lifting one leg with straight knee; other leg is flexed at knee, with foot on floor.

    d. Torso leaning slightly backward, with weight on hands extended behind; one leg extending with straight knee; other leg is extending forward on floor.

B. *Feel the difference when you lift two parts together.*

    1. Can you lift both legs in the air?

    2. Feel the weight in the middle of your body as you move as slowly and evenly as you can.

SOLUTIONS

    a. Lying on back, with arms along sides of body and legs elevating upward and slightly apart.

    b. Lying on back, with arms extending sideward, palms up, and legs extending in slightly diagonal position.

    c. Torso leaning backward, with weight on hands extended behind and legs extending in diagonal position, with knees slightly flexed.

    d. Torso leaning backward, with weight on base of spine, arms extending, legs extending in wide diagonal position, and knees straight.

    e. Sitting erect, arms and legs extending in diagonal position, as legs elevate, body curves slightly and weight shifts to lower back.

    3. Some of you are sitting and some of you are lying on your backs; this time begin from a sitting position. Are your movements lighter or heavier? Faster or slower?

C. *Find your sense of balance when you lift three parts of your body.*

IV.A.3b

IV.B

IV.B.2a,b

IV.B.2c

1. Stand up and shake out your legs. As you are moving, feel the weight in the middle of your body.
2. Move slowly, but use your own tempo to keep your balance.
3. Are you using more space than when you moved two parts of your body?

SOLUTIONS

a. Body plane forward, with torso leaning diagonally over standing leg, other leg extending sideward, and both arms in diagonal position over head.
b. Body plane forward, with torso leaning slightly over standing leg, other leg lifting from front of body, one arm parallel to extended leg, and other arm raised from shoulder.
c. Body plane forward, with torso leaning over flexed knee of front leg, other leg extending backward and upward, knee flexed, toes pointed, and both arms fully stretching from shoulders above head.
d. Body plane forward, with torso leaning diagonally over standing leg, other leg elevating sideward, knee flexed in curved position, arms extending sideward and flexed at elbows, and hands turned inward.
e. Body plane forward, with torso curved slightly forward over standing leg, other leg raised high, knee flexed, foot pointing toward floor, and arms curved downward at sides.

IV.C.3a

IV.C.3b

IV.C.3c

IV.C.3e

V

Problem V: To experience sustained movement through tension and resistance.

A. *Let's explore the feeling of pushing space.*

1. Stand in a big circle without touching each other. Push the air away from you on one side of your body in a steady, even movement.

   SOLUTIONS
   a. Body plane forward, with legs in wide lateral stride, knees flexed, toes forward, one arm extending from shoulder, elbow bent, hand flexed, head facing extended arm, and other arm at side of body.
   b. Body plane forward, with legs in wide stride, knees flexed, feet forward, upper torso slightly twisting to right side, both arms extending parallel toward right side, hands flexed, and head facing hands.

2. Now use the weight of your whole body to push the air as far as you can.
3. What parts of you will help you push further into space?

   SOLUTIONS
   (Pushing to left side.)
   a. With torso in diagonal position, leaning toward flexed knee of left leg; left arms extending forward; back leg extending fully, resting on ball of foot; right arm extending backward in diagonal direction; head facing toward left arm.

V.A.1

V.A.1

V.A.3

b. With body plane forward and torso in low crouching position, knee of left leg is fully flexed, with foot on floor; left arm extending diagonally from shoulder; right leg extending in diagonal position, resting on inside of foot; right arm is parallel to leg; and head is facing left arm.

4. You've put more space between your legs and that helps you push into space. Where do you feel the stretch in your muscles?

ADDITIONAL ELEMENTS Space: *range, level, body shape*; time: *slow tempo with even rhythm.*

B. *Now feel the difference between pushing space and pushing something solid.*

1. Take an easy walk around the room in all directions. When you pass someone, nudge them gently with your shoulder and continue walking.
2. Now walk again, and as you pass someone in front, on the side, or behind you, nudge them with a different part' of your body.
3. This time as you pass, push strongly against someone. While one is pushing, the other should try to keep your place; then move apart quickly and keep walking.

ADDITIONAL ELEMENTS Spatial relationships: *created by contact and by moving in different directions with others*; time: *rhythmic pattern of long and short, accented or unaccented beats created by pushing and walking.*

SOLUTIONS
(Even gentle pushing requires considerable control of balance and body weight; tendency is to push too hard causing other children to lose balance or collapse completely.) Initially, children may use only arms, hands, or shoulders to push against another's arm, shoulder, back, and buttocks.

4. Now work in partners; one of you push and the other resist; move together slowly and control your bodies so that you don't collapse.
5. There are other parts of you that are strong besides your arms and hands; feel the "push" in another part of your body.

SOLUTIONS
a. Hands against stomach, upper torso curving forward,

hands pushing against stomach of "resister," forcing him to move in backward direction.

b. Hands against back, torso is erect, hands extending from shoulders against partner's back; both moving in forward direction.

c. Stomach against stomach, impulse comes from center of body of "pushing" partner, back is arched, arms hanging from shoulders; one partner walking forward, one backward.

d. Stomach against back, similar to the previous solution, except both partners are walking in same direction.

e. Shoulder against shoulder, body planes of both partners are lateral, partner pushing with elbows flexed and arms close to chest to increase tension; both moving sideward.

f. Hip against hip, body planes of both partners are forward but spatial direction is sideward; hip of "pushing" partner is fully extending over straight leg, feet moving in cross steps; partner takes sliding steps.

g. Head against head, both partners lying on the floor; the "pushing" partner's face is downward; arms are flexed at elbows, propelling body forward; pushing partner lying on back, with knees flexed, feet on floor, and arms at sides.

ADDITIONAL ELEMENTS Space: *direction, level, range, body shape*.

C. *What is the opposite feeling of push? Explore the difference between pushing and pulling.*

1. Take your partners again or choose new ones; one of you will pull, the other will be pulled; then change.
2. Feel the weight come from the middle of your body so that you don't lose your balance by pulling too hard.
3. What parts of your body are you using when you pull? What parts of you are being pulled?

SOLUTIONS

a. Pulling by an elbow. Partners stand side by side, facing in opposite directions; inside arms are interlocked at elbows; opposite arms of "pulling" partner extending from shoulder for balance; both moving in wide, cross-step foot pattern.

b. Pulling by a foot. One person sitting on floor; one leg extending forward in air, the other leg is slightly elevated;

V.C.3d

hands are on the floor; "pulling" partner walking slowly backward, pulling extended foot with both hands.

c. Pulling by a leg. One person lying on side, with leg extended in diagonal direction; other leg is extended on floor; both arms are overhead; partner pulling body in forward direction by leg, keeping torso in lateral position.

d. Pulling through the arms. Both partners standing erect,

V.C.3e

facing each other; "pulling" partner grasps wrists of other person; as tension in the arms increases, "pulled" partner yields by curving upper torso forward, walking at middle level in space.

e. Pulling from the arms. Partners facing same direction; backs are curved at middle level in space; heads are downward; front person extending arms backward grasping

partner's hands, pulling in forward direction.
f. Pulling torso by the arms. Partners facing in opposite directions; torsos twisting in diagonal position; "pulling" partner pulls crossed arms of other person; twisting torso lower over flexed knee of forward leg; back leg is extended.

ADDITIONAL ELEMENTS   Spatial relationships: *range, level, body shape.*

UNDERSTANDINGS FOR TEACHERS—PROBLEMS IV–V

In problem IV, children must control different groups of muscles against the pull of gravity by finding ways of sustaining and balancing their body weight. By elevating two or three parts of the body at the same time, whether from a standing or sitting position, children sense that different parts exert different amounts of force, move at different rates of speed, and cover a greater or lesser range of space.

In problem V, children are experiencing different qualities of sustained movement first by creating tension within their own muscles (for example, pushing air), and then by responding to the resistance of a real object (for example, pushing and pulling each other). In working with partners in a push-pull relationship, children learn to adjust their output of energy through a balance of resistance and acquiescence.

Explorations in Percussive Movement

Problem I: To explore qualities of percussive movement in relation to sounds of percussive instruments.

A. *What do we mean by percussive instruments? What kinds of movements do we use to make them produce sounds? (Children's responses: Shaking, striking, hitting, beating.)*

1. There is a special family of instruments that just makes shaking sounds. What are those instruments? (Children's responses: Bells, maracas, tambourines, rattles, gourds.)
2. How am I playing this tambourine? (Shaking may elicit both striking and twisting movements. Beating may elicit sharp, staccato movements.)
3. When the tambourine is shaking, some of you are twisting different parts of your body. Let's explore that feeling together.
4. What parts of you can you twist when you are sitting down? Kneeling? Standing?

SOLUTIONS

Sitting, children begin by moving head, shoulders, and upper torso separately. Kneeling, torso twists from hips; arms are extended, increasing range of space. Standing, head, shoulders, hips, arms, and torso twist separately or in combination; torso uses greater range of space; arms twist down at sides, extended outward, or flexed at elbows; feet are stationary, together or in stride.

5. Now what parts of you can you shake? Can you start with one part, then two, then three, and finally shake your whole self?

   SOLUTIONS [2]
   a. Sitting on floor, with one knee flexed and foot on floor; other leg is elevated, with knee flexed, foot shaking, weight supported on opposite hand and foot; hand shaking on same side of body as elevated foot.
   b. Sitting on floor, with one leg extended forward and toe pointed, "shaking" leg is elevated and knee is flexed; arms are extending outward, with both hands shaking.

[2] Solutions to this problem may be seen in the film "Children Dance," produced and co-directed by the author and Naima Prevots. See bibliography.

c. Lying on back, with one leg slightly flexed; weight resting on heel; "shaking" leg is elevated and knee is flexed; arms are bent at elbows; shaking hands up in air.

d. Standing, with legs slightly apart; weight shifting from leg to leg as hips shake from side to side; arms are flexed at elbows; hands point downward.

e. Standing, with one knee flexed; other leg is straight and turned slightly sideward; torso bending at waist toward extended leg; one arm is flexed at elbow on same side of body; other arm has flexed elbow pointing upward; torso shaking from side to side.

ADDITIONAL ELEMENTS Space: *use of different body parts, increased range of torso and arms from sitting to standing position*; time: *different rhythmic patterns for different body parts, different tempos among children in standing positions.*

6. Let's give your movements a rhythm, just like the instrument. I'll shake and strike the tambourine in different ways and you follow; then you work out your own rhythms. (Teacher establishes definite rhythmic groupings in phrases of four of five measures.)

7. Divide in small groups and choose an instrument that you must shake to make a sound; play it first and listen to it; then pick up the feeling in your movement and let it take you through space. (Children may be divided into alternating groups of "players" and "movers.")

8. Some of you are playing maracas and some are playing bells. How do you move when you shake the bells? Fast? Slow? Are your movements big or little?

9. Make the bells dance with light, fast, shaking movements.

SOLUTIONS
Small, light staccato movements with hands, arms, feet, head; little use of torso.

10. Explore movements with the maracas in the same way. Can you shake them high–medium low? Can you turn while you are shaking different parts? Make a shaking dance as if there were maracas attached to every part of your body.

SOLUTIONS
Heavier, slower, striking movements than with the bells; each part of body produces jerky, relaxed, uneven movements; weight shifts from one leg to another, stepping or hopping; torso bends and stretches on different levels and in different

directions; more use of space in arms; greater use of directional space.

11. Let's have some people accompany with tambourines, bells, and maracas; the rest move in small groups to any instrument you wish; feel that the force of your movement is the same that produces the sound. (Each group moves separately with its own accompaniment.)

B. *There's another family of instruments that produces sounds by hitting or beating. What are those instruments? (Children's responses: Drum, claves, tone gourd, tone block, triangle.)*

1. Let's listen to the different qualities of sound made by these instruments; we'll have a small group play at a time; then we'll take turns.
2. Experiment with as many different ways of making sounds as you can. What kinds of movements are you making—heavy, light, even, uneven, loud, soft?
3. The rest of you move in twos and threes to the different sounds and rhythms that you hear. We will watch and see if we can tell what instrument you are moving with. (Children with instruments need to establish a consistent rhythmic pattern of long and short, accented or unaccented beats so that children moving will not be confused.)
4. *(To the players)* Do you use the same amount of force when you beat a drum as when you hit a triangle? *(To the movers)* Are your movements the same with the drum as with the triangle?

SOLUTIONS

Movements vary in quality from fast and heavy (drum), jerky and uneven (claves, tone blocks, claves) to light and fast (triangle). Both locomotor and body movements are used.

UNDERSTANDINGS FOR TEACHERS—PROBLEM I

Using instruments to reinforce percussive qualities lends another dimension to children's awareness that the energy which produces sounds also produces movement. Both "players" and "movers" need guided exploration in understanding this relationship and in being able to coordinate both elements. Emphasizing the difference between the drum and the triangle points to the contrast between fast and heavy (drum) and fast and light (triangle), as well as the gradations in between supplied by the other instruments.

*Working in terms of "families" of instruments helps children
understand that in relation to different sounds and varying degrees
of force, the body responds with different types of movements.
Twisting is an excellent example of the effect of force on a movement, that is, twisting percussively to maracas or a tambourine
produces one quality, whereas twisting in sustained movement
would completely change its expressive character.*

Problem II: To experience percussive qualities in terms of
heavy and light movement.

A. *Let's explore the feeling of moving fast and strong.*

1. Sit all tucked in or kneel on the floor; each time the drum
   beats, thrust a part of your body in space, as if you were
   poking a hole in the air; then quickly pull it back again.
   (Teacher plays heavy beats of relatively long duration with
   short pauses in between so that movements have a more
   thrusting than striking quality.)
2. You can use other parts of you besides your arms and hands;
   your legs, backs, and shoulders are strong, too. (Repeat previous rhythmic pattern.)
3. This time on every drum beat let each part of your body
   rise higher and higher until you are standing; then move
   back the same way, poking holes in the air as you go.

SOLUTIONS
Slow, jerky, angular movements, similar in quality to mechanical toys; responding to each beat by rising and lowering
requires control of body weight in coordinating the release of
energy in different parts.

ADDITIONAL ELEMENTS Space: *levels, range of body parts, body
shape*; time: *responding to rhythmic patterns, feeling the duration of fast, heavy beats.*

B. *Now feel the difference when you move fast and light.*

1. Take space on the floor; feel that you have strings attached
   to each part of your body, like a marionette.
2. Hang loosely for a moment, but don't collapse. Feel the
   string at each point so that you'll know where the pull will
   come from.
3. Move one arm quickly and sharply; each time you move it
   change its position in space; now move the other arm; move
   them together or in opposition.

4. Add your shoulders so that your movements become bigger; now move your head, arms, and shoulders as if the strings of your marionette are being jerked. (Teacher may accompany on drum, claves, tone blocks, and so on, to reinforce sharp, percussive quality.)
5. Let the strings drop and hang from your waist; relax the whole upper part of your body. Rest.
6. This time feel the strings pull from your hips, stomach, back, chest, knees, legs, and feet; start from your hips and move each part separately.

ADDITIONAL ELEMENTS   Space: *range of body parts, isolation of upper from lower torso; time: fast, staccato rhythm.*

7. Drop all the strings and hang over your legs, with your knees bent.
8. Now as you unfold, feel the strings pull quickly and sharply; keep your whole body moving in different directions and on different levels. (Simple percussive accompaniment may be found in *Rhythms Productions Records*, "Rhythm Instruments with Folk Music from Many Lands," Cheviot Corporation. See bibliography.)

Problem III: To explore the contrast in feeling between percussive and sustained movement.

A. *Let's explore the difference in feeling between moving slow and heavy and fast and light.*

1. Begin from any position and make a slow, heavy movement; you may lift a huge rock, or be a leaf falling, or feel like a heavy storm cloud.
2. Keep the movement going until you hear the drum signal to stop. (Teacher may play a long sustained sound on a gong or a steady series of light beats on a drum, and signal at an arbitrary point.)
3. At the signal, change the movement from whatever position you are in to fast, striking, light movements; continue until you hear the signal (maybe your rock has become a feather or your leaf is caught up in a fast wind, or your storm cloud breaks into rain). (Teacher gives exploration of percussive movement a sufficient amount of time so that child finds himself in a new and unusual position to begin the next experience.)

4. Now from where you are, feel the weight of your movements and end them as slowly and evenly as you can.
5. Let's watch each other and see if we can tell what kinds of images you were thinking about as you moved from one quality to another.

SOLUTIONS

Body shape: sustained movements tend to produce round, curved shapes, in body parts or in the torso; percussive movements appear more angular and asymmetrical; *space:* sustained movements are usually nonlocomotor movements, whereas percussive movements may be body or locomotor; *time:* sustained movements are of longer duration in an even, rhythmic pattern, whereas, percussive movements are of short duration in an even or uneven pattern.

UNDERSTANDINGS FOR TEACHERS—PROBLEMS II–III

In problem II, children are exploring percussive movements as force which begins abruptly and is stopped suddenly and quickly. In part B, isolation of the upper from the lower torso and articulation of small body parts allows children to experience the ways different parts of the body exert energy in space and time.

In problem III, contrast between fast and heavy and fast and light is an expression of the two polar elements of force—strong and weak. (Weak does not imply lacking energy, but expending relatively less energy to convey a particular movement quality.)

Explorations in Swinging Movement

Problem I: To experience swinging as an easy flow of energy initiated in different body parts.

A. *What parts of your body can you swing?*

1. Start very small; stand with your feet slightly apart and swing your head gently from side to side; let your ears touch your shoulders.

   SOLUTION
   Neck flexed and head forward and down, torso leaning forward from shoulders, head swinging from side to side in arclike path.

2. Swing your shoulders; feel your weight shift from one side to the other. What happens to your arms as you swing?

   SOLUTION
   Arms begin swinging at sides close to body; as impulse from shoulder becomes stronger, arms swing out in greater range of space.

3. Now let your arms carry your body in space.
4. What's the rhythm of your swings? Do it again and listen to the drum. (Teacher picks up 3/4 rhythms from those children who have established a regular pattern; as the movement continues, the rest of the group accommodates to that rhythm.)
5. So it's a "1, 2, 3" rhythm. On which beat are you using the the most force?
6. Now in big, easy movements swing your head, shoulders, arms, and the whole upper part of your body.
7. Some of you are bending at the waist and your arms are almost touching the floor; let's all swing lower and lower and lower.
8. What happens to your legs as you swing lower in space?

   SOLUTION
   As upper torso lowers, space between legs widens; body weight is centered in the middle; thighs open, with knees flexed outward.

B. *Your whole body is a swing; you are either sitting in it or being pushed in it.*

1. Where does it take you in space?

   SOLUTION
   Initial responses tend to be literal, like a "real" swing, that is, swinging forward and backward from a stationary position or moving forward and back, with small running steps.

2. What will help you swing higher when you are standing still?
3. Feel the air passing through your fingers and pass your face as you swing.

   SOLUTIONS
   a. Feet together, begin with small swings; arms are at sides; knees flex as torso raises and lowers.
   b. Feet together, torso swings forward and backward and knees flex; range of arms increases.
   c. Legs in wide forward stride, torso swings forward and weight balances on front foot; arms follow through in wide arc.
   d. In crouching position, arms swing forward and weight of torso shifts forward to balls of both feet, then returns to crouching position, in which knees are deeply flexed.

4. What parts of your body are you using now? In what directions are you moving?
5. When you swing as far as you can go, some of you almost fall out! How can you control your body and still make the swings big?

   SOLUTIONS
   Swinging the body backward and forward from a stationary base involves a continuous shift in body weight as torso, arms, and legs increase their range of space. Movements vary from small, arclike paths to large, rhythmic to-and-fro motions.

   ADDITIONAL ELEMENTS Space: *range, level, body shape;* time: *even, rhythmic pattern of groupings of threes.*

C. *Now let your swings take you through space. Swing up, swing down, swing side to side and around.*

   1. Feel the weight from the middle of your body so that your legs and arms can swing freely.

      SOLUTIONS
      a. Body plane frontal, arms in wide parallel position swing

sideways across upper torso, legs in wide stride; knees flex alternately as weight shifts from side to side.

b. Feet in wide stride pointing frontward, body plane twists laterally as arms swing across body from side to side; as weight shifts, opposite heel lifts slightly from floor.

c. Body plane frontal, as arms swing parallel from side to side across body, opposite leg extends and lifts from floor in diagonal position; as weight shifts, legs elevate alternately.

d. Body plane frontal, legs are in wide lateral stride and arms extend diagonally above head; as torso swings from side to side, legs elevate alternately.

e. Body plane frontal, arms swing sideways from shoulders; as weight shifts, legs rise alternately, stepping in zigzag, turning directions through space.

ADDITIONAL ELEMENTS Space: *direction, level, range, body shape;* time: *steady "1, 2, 3" rhythmic pattern in varying tempos.*

Problem II: To explore contrasts in qualities of force in swinging movement.

A. *Let's explore the feeling of swinging fast and light.*

1. Have you ever seen a grandfather's clock? What part of it

I.C.1d

swings back and forth? (Children may not know the word *pendulum*.)

2. Begin with little swings of a small pendulum using your heads. Feel the rhythm of the "tick-tock."
3. Keep your head moving and pick up the swing in one arm; now add your other arm and keep the rhythm going.
4. Where does a little swing take you in space? Are you using a lot of force?

I.C.1e

5. Listen to the rhythm of your swings; when you feel it, continue moving with it. (Teacher picks up 3/4 time from children, who have established a moderately fast tempo; beats lightly on drum so that children relate the amount of force to the rhythm.)

B. *Now feel the difference between swinging fast and light, and swinging slow and heavy.*

1. Your pendulum is in a much larger clock, so it takes longer to get from one side to another.
2. Begin with small, light swings again; as your body moves, feel the pendulum become heavier and heavier and swing further and further in space. (Teacher may accompany on percussive instruments, using two different qualities of sounds to reinforce contrast in force, for example, maracas, raspa, guiro for fast and light and gong, drum, cymbals for slow and heavy.)
3. Do the little swings take as much force as the heavy swings? Do they take as much time?
4. Feel the weight of the pendulum flow from the top of your head, to your shoulders, to your torso, to your legs; feel it from the middle of your body out through your arms.

SOLUTIONS

Heavy and slow movements produce a more sustained quality, with wider range of space of arms, legs, torso; tempo is slower than in percussive movement but rhythmic pattern remains in measures of three beats.

UNDERSTANDINGS FOR TEACHERS—PROBLEMS I–II

Exploring swinging movements in different parts of the body helps children become conscious that in each part, energy is released and controlled in different dimensions. They become aware that the force expended in small body parts exists in their own space–time relationship and that when the whole body is involved, the movements increase in range but may be of longer duration.

Coordinating body parts in swinging movement calls forth a sense of balance when the weight shifts, elevating a leg in space. In problems of this nature children experience the feeling of shifting the center of gravity.

In problem II, expressing different qualities within the same type of movement helps children build a broader vocabulary. The image of a pendulum is used to emphasize the contrast between the two qualities of force, but children may suggest other images that are equally appropriate.

Explorations in Vibratory Movement

Problem I: To experience vibratory movements as qualities of force which set the body into quick, small, quivering motions.

A. *Let's see what kinds of force we can use with instruments in the "shaking" family.*

1. Some of you choose those instruments which belong in that family. (Children select wrist bells, bells on sticks, maracas, gourds.)
2. People with instruments sit together; we'll take turns playing and watching.
3. Begin very slowly in any kind of rhythmic pattern you wish. What kinds of movements are you making to produce these sounds?
4. Now change the tempo; begin again slowly, then play faster and faster and faster until you can't shake anymore.
5. Move to the rhythm of your instruments and feel the changes as the "shakes" get faster.

SOLUTIONS

Shaking instruments, with hands together in front of body, above head, out to sides. Shaking serially, with hands alternating up and down, in and out, in circular motions; feet stepping, running, hopping on alternate feet, stamping with alternate feet as tempo increases.

6. Some of you are standing in one place and some are moving around. Let's have everyone take a wide stride and bend your knees; start shaking your hands with very quick, light movements and bring them up slowly until your arms stretch way over your head; come back down the same way. (Whole group explores this movement, with and without instruments.)

SOLUTIONS

Movement begins with fast turning and fanning of hands between the knees; as arms rise upward and outward, range of hands increases slightly but force remains the same; movements vary from fast shaking to vibratory.

7. For those of you who were shaking very quickly, what did the movements feel like? (Children's responses: fluttery, jiggling.)

B. *Let's explore this "fluttery" movement without instruments so you feel it in your muscles.*

1. Take space and see what parts of your body you can move in this way.
2. You can begin from any position—standing, kneeling, sitting, lying.

SOLUTIONS
Children move heads, hands, arms, feet in trembling, small, motions; energy level ranges from strong to weak, depending upon the part of the body involved.

3. Most of you are shaking so fast that you are really vibrating, just like a butterfly's wings.
4. What sorts of things do you do that might make your bodies move like that? (Children's responses: Shivering on a cold day; shaking off water after swimming; chattering teeth when you drink something cold.)

C. *Think of a butterfly's wings and feel that kind of movement in some part of your body.*

1. You know how light and gentle they are; see if you can put that quality into your hand.
2. Lift one hand and feel the wings flutter; now pick up a butterfly in the other hand.
3. Butterflies usually do not stay in one place, so watch them with your eyes and let the movements lead you through space. (Children need sufficient time to coordinate locomotor movements while focusing on the vibratory movements of the hands.)
4. Now bring them back from where you began; sit down and quickly let them fly away.

SOLUTIONS
Children move at different tempos, walking, running, sliding; arms moving slowly and fluidly in all directions in space (up, down, sideward, in and out, around), in contrast to hands, which move in quick, oscillating gestures.

ADDITIONAL ELEMENTS Space: *direction, level, range of hands and arms;* time: *fast tempo with staccato beats.*

5. Can you think of other things that make vibratory movements? (Children's responses: Machines, pneumatic drill, flicking a tight rubber band, humming bird's wings.)

Although vibratory movement is not used frequently by young children, it offers another quality through which to express a mood or idea in improvisations and dance studies.

In dance terms children are experiencing percussive movements that can be intensified by releasing energy more rapidly in small, explosive spurts. Because such movements require a unique kind of control, children are learning still another way to use their bodies.

IV

Expressive movement through imagery

11. *Concepts and explorations in imagery*

Conventional gestures and dance movement

Ideas for dance come to children most readily through imagery, which draws its expressive content from both real and imagined experiences. As such, they may be concrete or abstract and based on actual sensory experiences of seeing, feeling, hearing, touching, or imagined states of feeling, such as tender and quiet, wild and frenzied, mysterious and vague. In all cases, images in dance speak through the *qualities of movement* and should not be reduced to words or narrative gestures. The purpose of imagery as a catalyst for movement is not one of describing, but of *interpreting* feelings and phenomena which make up a child's "inner" and "outer" world. Perhaps this can best be clarified by Langer, who states, "What is expressed in dance is an idea; an idea of the way feelings, emotions, and all subjective experiences come and go. . . . What we call a person's 'inner life' is the inside story of his own history; the way living in the world feels to him." [1]

[1] Suzanne K. Langer, "The Dynamic Image: Some Philosophical Reflections on Dance," in *Aesthetics and Art*, Lee A. Jacobus (ed.) (New York: McGraw-Hill Book Company, 1968), p. 79.

It becomes clear, then, that the richest sources are drawn from children's own experiences, for they offer the most meaningful associations. However, for the most part, teachers tend to rely upon story books and to elicit literal representations of a particular role or situation. Because stories follow a sequential order, children are also expected to respond accurately to the story line in terms of the precise moment at which characters must appear, the duration of their part, and the similarity of their movements to the descriptions in the book. Although there is a close relationship between dramatic imagery and dance, in that both involve an identification with people, things, or activities, in dance, children imagine themselves in these states of being by abstracting only those qualities which they can best express in movement terms.

The point of departure is that children's dance is essentially improvisational (because we are not concerned with choreography), and although it may draw its stimulation from other art forms (poetry, music, song, drama), it speaks through its own image. The simple fact that stories are written in words and that dance is expressed in nonverbal movements tells us that we cannot merely translate from one form to another. What

IV: Expressive movement through imagery

distinguishes dance from other art forms is the unique use of space–time–force as aesthetic elements. Explored in innumerable combinations and in varying intensities, these elements give expressive qualities to a child's interpretation of movement, which transforms imagery from storytelling to dance.

In order to provide children with alternatives to imitative or stereotype movements, we must again consider the relationship between conventional gestures and dance movement. As was discussed in the first chapter, conventional gestures are those used in everyday behavior and must be universally understood to be communicated. The example given earlier of the waving of a hand to signify "hello" or "good-bye" applies here. In either of these, the combined use of space–time–force is typical of most gestures: space is usually limited to the immediate body area; time is generally of brief duration; and the amount of force varies with the utilitarian function of the gesture.

Dance movement, on the other hand, does not have to be directly communicative and universally understood in terms of its original source. Although it may stem from a common gesture, such as a greeting, the movement may begin in one hand, be repeated by the other, be carried into the shoulders and the head, and finally be broadened and exaggerated by the use of the whole body. Thus, because the movements are greatly increased in range and direction, it is given a more perceptible shape in *space*. In *time*, repetition may create a rhythmic pattern with a prolonged or accelerated tempo. The amount of *force*, instead of serving a functional purpose, may provide an additional emotional impulse by sharper contrasts in tension and relaxation and in strong or weak, heavy or light movements. As children experiment with space, time, force in elaborating gestures into dance movements, they discover that each can make of an experience his own emotional statement.

Dance and pantomime

From conventional gesture to pantomime is an easy transition, for the two share common features. Although dance and pantomime have certain similarities, there are marked differences which teachers frequently confuse in using dramatic imagery as motivation for movement. The most obvious similarity is that both pantomime and dance express ideas and emotions

218

without speech and use the body as the medium of expression. John Martin places the relationship between dance and drama in this way, "Dramatic form as such can be said to exist when dance, instead of presenting the essence of an emotional experience, deals with a specific sequence of events, out of which such an experience grows. The more literal its treatment, the less it has of dance about it." [2] He goes on to state that dance is distinguished from drama in that the "body reacts to all stimuli first in terms of movement, and that communicative movement suitable for dance can be drawn only from what might be termed [a] *motor memory of emotion*" [3] (my emphasis).

Pantomime as a dramatic form is frequently conceived of by children as "acting out," which they associate with directions to "pretend you are . . . a bunny, an airplane, Billy Goat Gruff." A vocabulary which includes such terms as *pretend* or *act as if* reveals the basic difference between acting *like* something or someone and expressing feelings *about* something

or someone. If, for example, children use animals in stories as sources of imagery, the intent is not to move *like* an elephant, a swan, or a giraffe. Rather, children must sense in their bodies the qualitative aspects of the movement by exploring the *shape* of the animal, the *weight* of its body as it moves through space, the use of *body parts* for different types of locomotion, and the feeling of moving in a special way.

By the same token, imagery drawn from phenomena in nature is not created from facts. A child cannot make a dance about the sun based on the number of light years it is from the earth, the degree of heat it radiates, or the composition of its rays. He can, however, create a dance study about his "inner feelings" toward the sun, and even about the movement of the whole solar system. Here again we are dealing with images as the translation of subjective experience into shaped feelings.

In contrast, when a child "acts out" a character in a story, his interest is to simulate that character as closely as possible. In so doing, he is attempting to represent someone other than himself. Movements in this case are designed for storytelling, and the focus is on their narrative, de-

[2] John Martin, *Introduction to the Dance* (New York: Dance Horizons, Inc., 1968), p. 84.

[3] Ibid., p. 86.

IV: Expressive movement through imagery

scriptive aspects. Thus, pantomime deals with the specific nature of a role or action which must be communicated and understood by an audience in terms of what is being done and who or what is doing it.

To return to the idea presented earlier, when children are searching for movement forms through which to organize their emotions and ideas, they are not pretending. They are attempting to sense the particular qualities of an image in relation to how it "feels" in visual–kinesthetic terms. The Haiku lends itself as a vivid illustration of adapting imagery from poetry. If, for example, a child abstracts the movements of a frog, a flower, and a butterfly, he is not *personifying* these characters, but he is bringing to bear his own emotional insight and dance vocabulary in creating a new form. What replaces the original poetic image is a distillation of the essence of the original idea, expressed in movements rather than words.

Metaphoric nature of imagery

If we are really to unleash children's imaginations, we must be aware that the function of imagery in dance is metaphoric, just as the total effect of the seventeen words in a haiku is sometimes a visual but always a *symbolic* image. Strictly defined, a metaphor is the connecting of diverse experiences by means of a symbol or image. In this instance, it is connecting the poetic experience of language with the experience of movement to produce thoughts or emotions expressed in a new way, in a formerly unrelated form. If, in our hypothetical haiku of a frog, a flower, and a butterfly, a child were to move *like* each of these as accurately as possible, the outcome would be exactly one frog, one flower, and one butterfly.

Although imagery frequently takes its sources from nature, in the sense of focusing on certain attributes or features, the metaphoric power of dance is that it reshapes nature's forms into movement forms. Thus, when children are released from inhibiting instructions, such as "move like that frog" or "move as the poem says," they are freed from literal mimetics to engage in the metaphoric process. At whatever level of complexity or sophistication, children can become involved in this process of exaggerating or eliminating, distorting or idealizing those elements that are given new forms and meanings through dance. It is not unusual, for example, that when children demonstrate an improvisation based on a haiku theme, the words have to be reread to establish the original meaning, for the qualities of the movement take on a life of their own.

Dance is neither acting nor pretending. Rather than representing movements through conventional gestures, dance *suggests,* and its "suggestiveness" implies that movement may have more than one meaning, depending upon how a child chooses to interpret it. At the same time, the interpretation of the movement is left open to the viewer, allowing him to make his own associations.

Expressiveness and meaning in dance

The emphasis here has been on the expressive qualities of movement, and is reflective of the question posed by Selma Jean Cohen as to whether dance is distinguished from other forms of movement (marching, ironing, simple repetition, pantomime) purely because of its expressiveness alone. (Although her query is directed toward dance as a mature art form, it has relevance for children's dance as well.) "The pantomime artist," she writes,

is even more expressive. By watching his movements we know exactly the kind of character he is representing, the

emotion he is feeling, even the particular action he is performing, such as opening a door or tying his shoes. We can justify by its literal meaning every one of his emotions. . . . The actions of the pantomime artist would seem to be more interesting because each of them has a meaning. But it is for this very reason that they differ from the movement of a dance. We watch the mime attentively in order to identify his actions; he is putting on his coat, now he is opening his umbrella. This is movement that has interest of meaning, but not interest above meaning. When we fail to understand the movements of the mime, we find no pleasure in his performance.[4]

Turning to dance, she states, "Dancing may be thought of as movement framed to be seen for its own sake and interest even above its interest and meaning."[5] What she is suggesting corresponds to the point made at the beginning of this chapter, that meanings emerge from the ex-

[4] Selma Jean Cohen, "A Prolegomenon to an Aesthetics of Dance," in *Aesthetics and the Arts,* Lee A. Jacobus (ed.) (New York: McGraw-Hill Book Company, 1968), p. 83.

[5] Ibid., p. 83.

pressive combinations of space–time–force (that is, the spatial relationships formed by the body, the rhythmic phrasing of the movements, and the changing, dynamic qualities of force). We may say, therefore, that expressiveness is based on a vocabulary of these elements which are the very fundamentals of movement itself.

Imagery in dance must have an action potential for movement. However, whether a child can create an image from an object or idea depends upon the strength of his own imaginative response to it, and the extent to which that object or idea has become a part of his general awareness. In selecting imagery, therefore, or in encouraging suggestions from children, teachers need to realize that objects, feelings, or events cannot be used metaphorically until they are sufficiently familiar in children's experience to have made an impact on their consciousness.

As has been noted, children draw from the sensory elements in their environment. They see, hear, touch, smell, and it is through these faculties that experiences and impressions are transformed in movement to create images in dance. The first step is to help children become sensitive and receptive to the sensory phenomena around them. When given an opportunity to explore them in relation to their own ideas, feelings, and moods (such as a walk outside to observe and absorb the landscape), we can help children gradually develop into "sensuously responsive" human beings.

Moving to textural qualities in the environment brings into focus experiences which children may have had but intensifies impressions of which they were only partially aware. For example, by exploring feelings of walking on a hot sidewalk, into cold water, through bushes, or over puddles, movement may be stimulated through the recall of tactile sensations. Hopping or jumping in different ways to avoid "being burned," pushing bushes away in long, sustained movements to find a path for walking through them, or experiencing "shivers" as vibratory movements helps children become aware that forms of feelings can find their expression through the elements of dance.

Calling upon a child's imagination to bring forth his own ideas opens his growing sensitivities to a new level of awareness. Direct, immediate experiences in everyday living also provide sources which are, in many ways, richer than vicarious experiences derived from books. By allowing a child's imagination to be the focus of imagery, we can introduce broadly defined situations which leave both the

222

problem and its exploration up to him. That is, a teacher may offer categories or areas of imagery which she feels are germane to the curriculum and will be of interest to her particular group. She may, for example, suggest the seasons of the year, because, having both sensory and narrative content, they may enrich a social studies program or simply may be enjoyed for their own sake.

It is in the way such ideas are presented that largely determines whether children's responses will take on improvisational or literal forms. Questions should be posed which allow for the widest imaginative possibilities, such as, "What are the special qualities of spring? Fall? What are the very special things that happen in winter? Summer?" Whether one season is chosen by the entire group or whether each child selects the one which has particular associations for him, the "story" or dramatic aspect emerges from within the improvisation of the movement itself.

As an example, in exploring the experience of water as a special phenomenon of summer, children discover that there is a distinct difference between moving with the flowing quality of water and being in water. Emphasizing the very special features of spring may elicit responses which depart from traditional practices of bun-

nies hopping, flowers growing, sun shining. As another vision, children may be inspired to search for the qualities of new life and growth that occur in the spring so that there is an interrelationship and continuity within the total image. On a more abstract level, textural qualities may be expressed through the forces of nature, such as thunder, lightning, smog, and wind, which bring forth striking contrasts in dynamics. (Because of the unpredictable content of imagery that would be appropriate for a given group of children, the explorations included in this chapter are more suggestive and less detailed than in the preceding sections.)

Teachers who wish to open possibilities of image making through dance must be aware that it is the aesthetic elements of space–time–force which function in both the conceptualization and presentation of imagery. To understand this is to realize that it is these very elements, viewed here as purely expressive qualities, which give any mode of imagery its form and excitement. Given such awareness, children can formulate their responses with the kind of richness and intensity that is inherent in dance.

Explorations in Imagery

Problem I: To explore categories of gestures used in everyday communication.

A. *Everyone uses different kinds of gestures to show how we feel about someone or something (emotional gestures).*

1. Sit together on the floor. Without using words, how would you say, "Come here"?

   SOLUTIONS
   Wiggling gesture with index finger; slight scooping gesture of one hand; waving motion toward body with forearm and hand.

   a. Can you say it with your head? Your shoulders? Your feet?

   SOLUTIONS
   Head nodding in short percussive movements toward opposite shoulder; shoulder contracting and releasing toward center of body, or, with greater impulse from shoulder producing a swinging gesture of arm; leg extending in air or resting on floor; toes flexing and releasing in staccato movements.

2. How would you ask the person next to you to "Give me some"?

   SOLUTIONS
   One hand or both hands extending with palms upward; arm flexing at elbow close to body, palm upward.

   a. Can you ask with the whole upper part of your torso?

   SOLUTIONS
   From a sitting position, torso bending at waist; with head and shoulders forward; both arms extending with palms outward. Sitting cross-legged, one arm extending sideward; torso bending toward arm; weight shifting to leaning side, pulling knee of opposite leg slightly off floor.

3. How would you tell someone to "Go away!"?

   SOLUTIONS
   Pushing outward with forearms; with elbows flexed close to body; striking with one arm backward and forward in repeated, percussive movements; swinging arm in arclike path

from center of body outward; pushing with arms in parallel position from shoulders from one side to the other.

4. When you feel very strongly, what gestures do you make to say, "Stop! "No, no, no!"

SOLUTION
Movements are initially limited to arms and hands within close spatial range of the body.

5. Let's do each group of words together so that we can see how each person "speaks" in different movements. (After a period of exploration, teacher may pick up each child's

I.A.3

pattern on the drum to reinforce individual rhythmic groupings.)

6. Is there a rhythm to what you're saying? Do certain words have different qualities of space and force? Begin again with the small gestures that you used and exaggerate them by changing the space, the time, and the force. (Teacher accompanies both patterns, emphasizing accented beats to make children aware of the difference between gestures and dance movements.)

7. Now explore these gestures using your whole body; take space on the floor and move in any direction and on any

level; repeat each one three times. (Accompanying each grouping in three measures gives children a sense of phrasing.)

8. It's not necessary to make faces; we should be able to tell whether you are sad, happy, angry, or frightened by the way you use your bodies.

SOLUTIONS

Rhythmic patterns. Long and short beats.

"Come here"	—— –	(long, short)
	– ——	(short, long)
"Give me some"	– – –	(short, short, short)
	—— – –	(long, short, short)
	– —— –	(short, long, short)
"Go away!"	—— – –	(long, short, short)
	– – ——	(short, short, long)
"Stop!"	——	(long)
	–	(short)
"No, no, no!"	– – ——	(short, short, long)
	– – –	(short, short, short)

(Tempo varies from slow to fast. Long and short beats give feeling of measures.)

Spatial patterns. Children begin from all positions (that is, sitting; kneeling on one leg, or on both; rising from a kneeling to a standing position; lowering from a standing to a crouching or kneeling position—e.g., "come here"; *locomotor movements:* walking, running, or lunging—e.g., "go away"; *body movements*—twirling, twisting, with explosive movements of arms and hands—e.g., "stop"; bending and stretching—e.g., "give me some."

Force. Amount of tension varies with the expressed emotional intent ranging from heavy, sustained movements (for example, "come here," "give me some"), heavy or light percussive movements (for example, "go away," "stop"), to percussive or vibratory movements (for example, "No, no, no").

B. *There are certain kinds of gestures that we always use with other people (social gestures).*

1. Can you say hello to someone when you meet them, without using words?

2. Take an easy walk around the room with the drum; when it stops, greet the person nearest you; when the drum starts, continue walking.

SOLUTIONS

While children initially may shake hands, the exact nature of the gesture will vary according to the age and background of any particular group.

3. Now run lightly with the drum; when it stops, greet another person without touching them; then run until it stops again. (Repeat several times.)
4. Some of you made motions with other parts besides your hands. This time greet your friends with different parts of your body; if you touch someone, make sure that you don't knock them over.
5. What parts of you did you use? (Children's responses: Head, body, back, elbow, knees, hips.)
6. Did you use the same amount of space and time as when you just shook hands? How did you use your energy this time?
7. Divide into small groups and make a "gesture" dance; think about greeting someone small, tall, skinny, fat, or however you imagine each other.

SOLUTIONS

Children respond to each other kinesthetically, giving and taking movement cues which emerge from the abstractions of the gestures themselves. All elements are involved: *space*—direction, level, range, body shape, focus; *time*—repetition of gestures in accented and unaccented beats, accommodating to each other's tempo; *force*—flow and control of energy, depending upon extent to which gestures are abstracted into dance movement.

C. *Sometimes you make gestures when you are all alone and no one is around (gestures for self-communication).*

1. What are some of the motions that you make just for yourselves? (Children's responses: "Itching" your nose, twirling a piece of your hair, scratching yourself.)
2. Think of something that you do and begin with a very small gesture.
3. What parts do you use mostly? (Children's responses: Hands, arms, head.)

4. Now make these same movements bigger and stronger and feel the difference in the way you use your body.

SOLUTIONS

Scratching. Beginning with small scratching gesture on one shoulder; other hand scratching opposite side; then both hands scratching in rapid movements up and down and around body, producing twisting, bending, and stretching of torso; feet hopping up and down alternately; movements increase in range, tempo, and intensity, giving whole body movement a jerky, percussive quality.

UNDERSTANDINGS FOR TEACHERS—PROBLEM I

In this problem, children become aware that gestures are acts of expression for the purpose of communicating ideas or feeling to others or to the self. When they are communicated to others as nonverbal signs, they are meant to be interpreted by someone else. When they are used as self-expressive communication, it is the person telling himself.

In part A, emotional gestures are based primarily on one's needs or feeling states in relation to another person; in part B, social gestures are derived from conventional patterns in everyday behavior based on expected responses of others; in part C, gestures for self-communication are directed inward and function on a purely sensory level.

By consciously elaborating and exaggerating through different combinations of space–time–force, children experience how these gestures are transformed into dance movement.

Problem II: To explore the movement qualities of imagery drawn from various areas of the curriculum.

A. *What are some of the special things that happen in different seasons of the year?*

1. Divide into groups. Decide on a season that you particularly like and explore the special things about it.
2. You are not going to "tell a story," but "dance a story" about whatever season you choose. Then we'll watch each group separately. (The time allotted to these improvisations will vary; they may be demonstrated at the end of one session or after several dance periods.)
3. In the spring, for example, what are the new things that are

born? What is their size—their shape, their weight? How do they move? Feel these qualities in your own body.

4. In the winter how do you walk in the snow? How does an icicle melt? What are the shapes of icicles? What is the shape of a snowman?

5. In the fall what happens to the leaves? Are all leaves the same shape? How strong is the wind? How do the branches look?

6. In the summer what do you do? Are you swimming in the water? Do you feel the waves? How hot is the sun? What kinds of shells do you find on the beach?

II.A.5

SPRING: SOURCES OF IMAGERY

a. Animals emerging from hibernation (for example, bears, snakes, fieldmice, ground hogs).

b. New growth (for example, flowers, grass, trees, birds, butterflies, rabbits).

c. Forces of nature (for example, gentle breezes, warm sun, light rain).

SOLUTIONS

(Trio.) First child standing erect, with arms raised above shoulders and elbows flexed, fingers spread apart, pointing upward (tree). Second child standing at right angle to first child, with arms fully extended from shoulders in diagonal position, "radiating" rays by slowly twisting torso from side to side (sun). Third child is curled up on floor, somewhat away from partners; he unfolds, wiggling on stomach in undulating movements to bottom of "tree," slithering slowly up back of first child until both arms are extended, with hands clasped above top of "tree," wiggling like a "snake's head."

MOVEMENT STORY   A *snake crawls out of its hole and crawls up a tree while the sun shines.*

SOLUTIONS

(Trio.) First child as a bean plant crouches on floor, with heels raised and weight on hands and balls of feet. Second child bending forward over "bean," with legs in wide stride and arms extending in wide arc, enclosing "bean." Third child facing second in same forward, in curved position (both leaves); as "bean" slowly rises, shifting weight to center of torso, arms rise from floor, flexing at elbows with hands together pointing upward. As "bean" grows, first and second child rise in same tempo, extending arms sideward in wider arcs to allow "bean" to push upward.

MOVEMENT STORY   A *bean plant grows out of two halves of a pod.*

FALL: SOURCES OF IMAGERY

a. Leaves falling from trees, different shapes of leaves.

b. Walking through piles of leaves.

c. Birds migrating in flocks.

d. Forces of nature (for example, heavy rain, strong winds, hurricanes, tornadoes).

SOLUTIONS

(If the season is actually Fall, each child brings in a leaf.)

a. From standing position, children drop leaves slowly and observe

how they fall in space—fast, slow, straight, zigzag, heavy, light?
  b. Each child explores the movement quality of his own leaf in terms of its *shape* (pointed, round, long, angular); *weight* (heavy, light); *space* (path, range); *tempo* (fast, moderate, slow).
  c. Observe the shapes of leaves when they are on the ground. "Dropping" and "falling" must be controlled in terms of balance and shift of body weight.

SOLUTIONS

(Trio.) First child standing with knees slightly flexed, one arm raised above head with fingers curved, torso bending slightly in opposite direction from extended arm (leaf). Second child standing beside first child, with legs in sideward stride, knees flexed, upper torso curving diagonally away from partner, arms flexed at elbows, forearms in angular shapes, fingers pointing downward, head leaning sideward following bend of torso. Both "leaves" falling in slow, collapsing movements, resting on backs, with knees fully flexed, arms flexed at elbows close to body. Third child approaches with wide, side-to-side swinging movements; as "leaves" are "swept," they roll over and over on torso, with knees flexed and feet in air. When "sweeping" stops, leaves are still.

MOVEMENT STORY *Two leaves fall from a tree and rest on the ground; someone comes along and sweeps them up.*

SOLUTIONS

(Group of eight.) Four children standing back to back (trunk); arms are in angular shapes, interlocking but not touching (branches). Fifth child runs around tree, rising and lowering torso with light, circular movements of arms (breeze); branches waving gently. Sixth child runs around tree, swinging arms in parallel and opposite directions in combinations of sustained and percussive movements (strong wind); branches swing from side to side. Seventh child runs around tree; arms are extended frontward and sideward in chopping movements; as he approaches each child, one branch collapses in a sharp, percussive movement. Eighth child runs around tree making chopping, striking movements of arms in up and down, sideward directions (hurricane); whole tree collapses.

MOVEMENT STORY *A tree stands alone, waves gently in the breeze. A strong wind shakes the branches; a stronger wind comes and makes the branches crack; a hurricane sweeps along and the tree falls.*

WINTER: SOURCES OF IMAGERY
a. Icicles hanging, melting.
b. Walking in deep snow; walking or skating on ice.
c. Making and throwing snowballs; making oneself into a snow-man.
d. Forces of nature (for example, snow, melting snow, snow-flakes).

SOLUTIONS
a. Children walking in different ways in a light snow (for example, small steps, gliding, sliding); snowflakes fall on their eyes, nose, head, shoulders, hands (to establish light quality of movement).
b. Snowflakes falling harder, becoming heavier and thicker; chil-dren walking through deep snow, feeling the weight on their heads, backs, shoulders; steps becoming higher or wider; tempo and force changing.
c. Children falling in the snow (on signal from drum or other instrument), continually rising and moving (to experience col-lapse and recovery as qualities of force).
d. Some children shovelling, others rolling in snow (gong, cym-bals, xylophone for glissando or rolling effect).

SUMMER: SOURCES OF IMAGERY
a. Swimming in water; moving as water in river, ocean, waterfall.
b. Walking on hot sand, into cold water, in puddles.
c. Making shapes of sea shells, sea creatures, fish, boats.
d. Moving as forces of nature (for example, hot sun, cool breeze, waves).

SOLUTIONS: SENSORY IMPRESSIONS
(Teacher may stimulate movement by suggesting word pictures.)

Walking in hot sand (Small groups.)
"It's summer now and you are walking on the beach; the sun is getting very, very bright and the sand is getting hotter and hotter with each step you take."
a. Children begin with a slow, relaxed walk; on cue of "hotter and hotter" tempo increases; locomotor movements change from walking, to small running steps, to leaping, to slapping feet off floor, to hopping on one foot for several beats and then on the other.
b. Children's responses fall into various ways of hopping: with in-creased lifting of feet, opposite leg is raised behind, with knee flexed, heel almost touching buttocks; alternate foot is held by both hands in front of body to express feeling of being

"burned." Child hops in circular direction, with increasing elevation, as if to "get off" the sand.

c. Children experience the feeling that a simple walk is too limited for the type of sensory expression they are seeking.

Movement of waves (Whole or small groups.)
"The waves in a river or a swimming pool give you one kind of feeling; the waves in the ocean are very different. What kinds of shapes do waves make? Let each part of your body flow so that you feel all 'watery'."

a. Start with small, gentle waves; let them flow from your head, to your shoulders, to your arms, to your legs. (Children should be encouraged to begin from positions in space other than the traditional one of crawling on the stomach.)

b. Now let the waves flow out of the middle of your body and feel them ripple in each muscle of your shoulders, arms, hands, legs, feet. Can your waves carry you down the river?

c. You have flowed into the ocean. Now your waves are pushing and pulling, rising and falling, getting big and bigger, small and smaller. (The feeling is one of changing the flow and control of energy to correspond to the different qualities of waves.)

UNDERSTANDINGS FOR TEACHERS—PROBLEM II, PART A

The "movement stories" of the seasons are stated in simple and direct terms as they are frequently described by children in "explaining" their ideas. The intent is to indicate that the "story" does not have to be elaborate or literal to provide a source for movements which may, of themselves, be very inventive and unusual.

In using sensory impressions as sources of imagery, word pictures are essentially related to tactile sensations, one of the primary modes of perception of young children. By heightening their sensitivity to these aspects in the environment, children are learning to select and abstract certain feelings and to find expression for them through movement forms. Whatever thoughts and feelings children wish to express, however, must be "felt" within the whole body so that the tactile sensations are combined to form a total visual–kinesthetic image.

Problem II

B. **Science** *All the planets move in their own space, so we can "dance" the solar system.*

1. What is the center of the solar system? (Children's responses: Sun.) Does it shine in only one direction? How does it send out its heat and light? (Children's responses: Rays.)
2. Does the earth turn itself as it goes around the sun? Do all the planets move around the sun?
3. How does the moon move around the earth? Is it closer to the earth than the sun?
4. Let's have the sun in the middle and the rest of you take places around it where the planets might be.

SOLUTIONS

(Group of fourteen.) Four children standing back to back, with arms extended diagonally from shoulders, fingers stretched apart (sun). One child is "Mercury" (smallest planet); running with upper torso curved forward, arms curve forward, clasping elbows, head faces downward, he runs in close circles around the sun. "Earth" standing with arms in elongated curve above head, moves in three ways around the sun, turning in slow walking steps, bending torso diagonally in a circular path toward each part of the sun to indicate the four seasons, spinning on its "axis." "Moon," with arms curved sideward in downward position, twirls in circular path around the earth. "Saturn" turns slowly in center of "ring" formed by four children holding hands, moving in opposite direction. Two children as "Jupiter" (largest planet) extend arms, clasping wrists, turning in circular path. "Pluto," at farthest end of solar system, crouches with flexed knees, torso curved forward, arms encircling knees, stepping and turning in inward and outward direction in relation to sun.

C. **Special Studies** *All the things that Indians do in their daily lives have very special movements.*

1. Do men and women do the same things?
2. How do they get their food? Who gets the food? Who prepares it? How do they cook?
3. You are all one big "tribe," but work in small groups. Decide who you are and let your movements tell us how you are feeling about what you are doing.
4. Explore the most important ideas in the activities that you choose. Think of the shapes, sizes, weights of the things that you're doing. Perhaps some groups will need to work together.
5. Let's observe the activities that you have chosen.

II.C.6 *Festival*

SOLUTIONS

Men hunting, carrying animals on poles, fishing, chopping trees. Women cooking, weaving, sewing, planting, hoeing, tending the fire, carrying firewood on head and back.

6. Now that you have worked so hard, let's have a festival. How would you celebrate the rain, the growth of new crops, the fire that protects you and keeps you warm?
7. Can you make a "rain dance," a "planting or harvest dance," a "fire dance"? Use whatever instruments you wish; you can even make a "sounds dance."

D. Transportation *You have taken trips to airports, harbors, railroads, and you know that there are many ways of traveling.*

1. If you wanted to go a long distance in a short time, how would you go? (Children's responses: Airplane, jet, space ship.)
2. Use the whole dance area for your airport and remember that each moving thing needs its own space.
3. You need to be aware of how you are moving in relation to others around you, whether they are moving or not.

SOLUTIONS

(Group of eight.) Four children standing in a line, with torsos

II.C.7
Rain dance

II.C.7
Harvest dance

(a)

(b)

(c)

curved forward, arms and legs fully extended, hands almost touching floor (hangars). Four children are under "hangars," crouching on flexed knees, with torso bent forward over knees and arms fully extended sideward (planes). Two children are back to back on chair; each kneels on one knee and has arms flexed at elbows, raised in right angles, moving in arclike path from side to side (radar). Two children turning slowly around perimeter of room, with arms elevated above head, rotating hands in opposite directions (helicopters). "Planes" slowly emerge from hangars, rising to standing position with arms extended sideward; as tempo accelerates, torso tilts slightly from side to side to avoid hitting or bumping into wings of other planes. After circling airfield several times, planes decelerate tempo, lower in circular movements, and slide backward under "hangars."

4. Now let's travel by water. This whole area is the harbor.
5. Are all the boats the same? Do they move in the same way? What shapes are they?
6. Boats have a "home," just like airplanes. Where do they start their trips from in the harbor?
7. Do the ocean liners move out of their docks by themselves? Who helps them?
8. What "tells" the boats by its movement where the water is too shallow?

SOLUTIONS

(When desks are placed against the walls, children can move out from one or two sides of the room.) (Group of twelve.) Five children lie on their stomachs, with legs partially under desks, arms fully extended forward, and fingers together pointing in "prow" shape (ocean liners or freighters). Five children approach, with torsos bent over flexed knees, sliding on floor, with arms extended forward and flexed at elbows, close to knees, and hands together in pointed shape (tug boats). One child in middle of "ocean," stands with legs in wide lateral stride; with arms elevated above head, and hands pointing upward, swaying from side to side (buoy). One child stands on desk, with both arms extending forward from shoulders, palms touching, turning slowly from a fixed position (light house). Each tug begins from a different place and backs slowly toward an ocean liner. As tugs back in, "prows" of ocean liners open to grasp "feet" of tugs, both pulling in slow, sustained movements. As ocean liners are pulled toward center, tugs disengage and return to "docks" in rapid, percussive movements. Ocean liners glide on stomachs, with weight centered in arms and shoulders, pulling torso and legs in forward, rocking movements; they move in different directions, in wide, circular paths around "buoy"; as they head toward their own dock, tugs move out and pull them in. (Other types of boats suggested by children may include sailboats and row boats.)

UNDERSTANDINGS FOR TEACHERS—PROBLEM II, PARTS B–D

The problems suggested here, are examples of ways in which improvisations or dance studies may be related to other aspects of the curriculum. It is assumed, however, that the content selected is either based on children's general knowledge or experience or derived from a specific area of study.

In part B, for example, the intent is not to reproduce the actual "facts" of the solar system. The importance is in having children experience the interrelationship of each one's movement to another within a defined space, so that the total composition produces a bigger feeling than if each child were working alone. That is, although each child uses space–time–force differently, according to the way he conceives his movement, the effect is one of a unified feeling with those around him.

In part C, the assumption is that the children have studied an Indian tribe, but this problem can be applied as well to any community of people in terms of producers, consumers, services, family living, and so on. As in the previous problem, the purpose is not to imitate "real" activities, but to express, through movement, the feeling of people in their working relationships. For this reason, asking children to create their own "festival" relieves them from attempting to simulate literal references found in books or pictures. In this way movement ideas are developed first as expressions of feelings, out of which a dance study may take form.

The same approach is used in part D. Children create the forms of an image out of generalized ideas and experiences, which become reformed and reshaped in relation to the movements of others. In these types of interrelated group experiences, an individual's expression becomes intensified and enlarged because he is able to share in the varied contributions of other children as well as in his own self-discovery.

Problem III: To explore moving objects in the environment that lend themselves to imagery.

A. *There are machines all around us that move in different ways.*

1. Think of the machines that you use or that move in your house.
2. Your movements will show the kind of work your machine does. (Children move alone or in small groups.)
3. Think of your machine in terms of its size, its shape, its weight, its speed, and the parts that make it move.

SOLUTIONS [6]

a. *Meat chopper.* (Single child.) Standing, and with feet together, arms forward and parallel, elbows flexed and close to sides of body, moving forearms up and down in short, percussive movements.

b. *Popcorn machine.* (Four children.) Crouching on hands and knees and rotating in small circles, each child jumps up at different intervals in fast, staccato movements.

c. *Ice chopper.* (Single child.) Standing with feet together, arms fully extended, palms facing inward, moving arms alternately up and down in sharp, percussive movements.

d. *Toast popping in the toaster.* (Trio.) Two children facing each other; holding hands and crouching with flexed knees, heels off floor, arms extended forward. Third child crouching low, with feet on floor, arms encircling knees, head down; jumping up and down in rhythmic intervals.

e. *Steam rising in the kettle.* (Partners.) First child standing with torso curved forward from hips, arms extending sideward in wide arcs, and pointing downward with head facing down (kettle). Second child leans with torso curved over back and shoulders of partner, with arms extended forward; as "kettle" rises slowly, lifting torso to upright position, "steam" rises as arms extend upward.

f. *Clothes in the washing machine.* (Partners.) One child standing with torso curved forward, head and arms downward enclosing "clothes"; partner crouching in low position on knees under "machine"; weight shifts to palms of hands and pushing action of hands causes knees to pivot, turning body in circular direction.

4. What are some of the smaller "gadgets" that you use in the kitchen? (Children's responses: Egg beater, scissors, mixmaster, rolling pin, cookie cutter.)

[6] These solutions may be visualized in the author's film "Children Dance" (see bibliography).

III.A

III.A.3b

ARISE FROM SLEEP, OLD CAT
AND WITH GREAT YAWNS
AND STRETCHING . . .
AMBLE OUT FOR LOVE
Issa, p. 13

244 *IV: Expressive movement through imagery*

LIGHTNING FLASH, CRASH
WAITING IN THE
BAMBOO GROVE
SEE THREE DEW-DROPS FALL
Buson, p. 18

V

*Dance as knowing,
doing, and valuing*

12. *Expectations for teachers and children*

When we consider an assessment of children's performance in dance in terms of expectations, we are raising two fundamental questions: What do children have to *know* in order to do? What do children have to *do* in order to know?

In any creative endeavor, and specifically in dance, there are three common areas of experience—*knowing, doing,* and *valuing.* Although each may function to a greater or lesser degree in any given situation, they interact simultaneously in an on-going process. For this reason it is difficult to specify a sequence, for they are inextricably related and each one may become dominant at any particular time in the discovery process.

It is interesting that the intent of the questions posed above was raised by John Martin over thirty years ago, in some rather critical observations of the relationship of dance to education at that time. He writes,

The dance as a basic educator, along the lines of theory that treats the individual as an integer, is obviously unique, for no other activity calls into play the three departments of the personality with such equality of emphasis and especially such unity of impulse. This latter consideration is what is most frequently neglected, and we find the common systems of education tending to pull the individual apart instead of to put him together. He is trained to exercise his reasoning powers in one department, his muscles in another, and his capacity for feeling not at all. . . .[1]

He concludes that if the intellect seems to be underestimated in dance, it is not because it does not function actively, but because its role has been misunderstood. "It functions," he explains, "in terms not of pure intellection, but of applied intellection, as a link between feeling and action."[2]

With few exceptions, this fragmented approach to the education of the individual still prevails, and thus it becomes even more poignant to place expectations in proper perspective. If we recognize that knowing–doing–valuing constitute a complex and interdependent process, we might give thoughtful consideration to the question quoted by Bruner in "The Process of Education" of "How do I

[1] John Martin, *Introduction to the Dance* (New York: Dance Horizons, 1965), p. 290. (A Dance Horizons Republication.)

[2] Ibid., p. 291.

V: Dance as knowing, doing, and valuing

know what I think until I feel what I do?" [3] Although children do not conceive of this question consciously, we must be aware that within the very nature of the dance experience, they are living it.

In teaching any art form, we are ultimately concerned with increasing children's sensibilities as well as their abilities; thus, expectations are based on the promise that all children can achieve some degree of success and some level of creative attainment. Because our purpose is not one of training young children to become practicing dancers, criteria fall within two broad categories: the *level* and the *quality* of participation. We are concerned with a child's general participation in the dance program and with the quality of his problem-solving abilities.

Participation, as used here, partially implies the notion of "self-startingness" as well as active involvement, and might provoke some thought as to how the degree of "self-startingness" may change a child's level of ability. With regard to general considerations, four questions are suggested:

1. Do all the children participate all the time?

[3] Jerome Bruner, *The Process of Education* (New York: Random House, 1960), p. 30.

2. Do some children participate more frequently?
3. Do some children initiate more ideas than others?
4. Do some children go beyond the problem either in formulating new problems for themselves or in creating new solutions?

All paths of discovery move along uneven and sometimes inconsistent lines. Teachers must realize therefore, that not all aspects of the dance program may be of interest to all children, nor will all new movements be necessarily creative. Because there is no concept of failure within the conceptual framework presented here, each child must be judged according to where he is at any point in his creative growth, and not from where we wish he might be. Thus, if some quality of dance movement occurs that is new to him in his search for expressing ideas and feelings and shows development in relation to where he was in the beginning, that is more important educationally than whether that response has ever occurred before. It is perhaps also important to recognize that children do not have to explore every aspect of a problem with every possible variation in order to express the essential qualities of dance. Moreover, they do not have to achieve maximum body control before they can produce exciting dance movements. It is to be expected that if a dance program is designed with a broad range and diversity of materials, such as the one offered in this book, some children may respond to it completely and some may not. What is interesting for teachers is to observe which children relate to what problems, with the understanding that there is more than one approach to self-discovery.

The second criterion, which is based on a child's problem-solving abilities using movement as the medium, is more difficult to discern. However, growth and success in problem solving become the measure of impact for both children and teacher and are the justification for the inclusion of dance education in the general curriculum. Although this program is not presented within a total curriculum design, the basic concepts that have been formulated serve as connective tissue to give a sense of continuity to the total learning experience. Within this structure, therefore, each exploration or improvisation may be assessed existentially (that is, in the "doing") as well as retrospectively (that is, in terms of a child's unfolding development).

An individual's teaching style is probably more closely related to a child's performance in the arts than in any other area of the curriculum, because it is conveyed through attitudes and values rather than skills and techniques. Therefore, the problem of making qualitative judgments of a child's problem-solving abilities raises two pertinent questions: What do we want children to be able to do? How can we most effectively guide their learning? What we are suggesting is that a consideration of expectations must include teachers as well as children.

Teachers represent great diversity in understanding and ability both in relation to dance and to general teaching, and we must appreciate the fact that dance may be introduced in the classroom through diverse teaching styles, attitudes, and approaches. There are, however, two common factors which must enter into expectations for teachers: an understanding that dance as an art form embodies both process (how it is created) and product (what is created) and an ability to grasp the basic concepts through which creative problems may be extended.

In an area such as dance, where learning does not follow a logical systematic progression, a teacher is faced primarily with the need to know how and what to look for and to communicate in movement terms what she perceives. For teach-

V: Dance as knowing, doing, and valuing

ers, judging the qualitative aspects of a child's problem-solving abilities implies a capacity for self-evaluation in the same way that we encourage children to become both performers and critics of their own work. The difference is that once children are engaged in the dance process, they enter into it with few preconceptions of what is "right" or "wrong," "good" or "bad" (TV not withstanding). A teacher's own experiences may have produced impressions and even biases as to what children's dance should "look like" or "be," and the problem, then, becomes one of detaching herself from her own preconceptions of dance. Stated simply, the question is, how can we dissociate ourselves from precast standards so that we can observe children freshly? It is not that we teach in the absence of standards, but that given a broad conceptual framework, the nature of judgments must be made in terms of what children bring to the situation and what they are able to do within it.

Teachers may inhibit their own improvisational talents if they deal only with prior conceptions of what constitutes "right" and "wrong" ways of dance. In this sense, we are suggesting an approach that is nonjudgmental. On the other hand, there is a need for judgments based on criteria drawn from the inherent elements of the experience itself. In this way it becomes possible to frame questions which apply to a specific exploration as well as to a whole semester's work, such as:

1. Was the underlying concept clearly presented?
2. How were the ideas communicated in movement terms?
3. What kinds of solutions were observed in relation to the original problem (for example, use of space, time, force; movement alone, in couples, trios, and groups)?
4. Did the formulation of the problem lead to individualized solutions?
5. What was the teacher's role in the presentation of the problem (for example, overly directive and talkative, overly permissive, detached but involved, able to anticipate solutions and give support when needed)?

Such an approach allows teachers to set expectations which emerge from an intuitive, inductive process of knowing and feeling and which encourages their own self-awareness.

As has been stated earlier, expectations for children are considered in terms of what we want them to achieve as a result

252

of engaging in the dance experience. What we desire for children is essentially twofold: to develop a kinesthetic awareness of their ability to use their bodies expressively through dance forms and to develop a movement vocabulary which will verbally reinforce their kinesthetic responses. The following suggested criteria for qualitative judgments are at best tentative, but at least directly reflect the conceptual framework in which children's dance has been conceived.

First, *within the basic elements of space, time, force,* children are able to: (1) perceive them as the basic elements of dance, (2) identify these elements on a kinesthetic and verbal level, (3) become actively involved with these elements through dance problems, (4) relate these elements to their own attitudes and experiences.

Second, *within the total construct of space, time, force,* children are able to (1) differentiate and discriminate among the movement elements, (2) understand the total structure as it relates to their own organization and patterns of movement, (3) perceive these elements as aesthetic qualities in relation to their own explorations and improvisations, and (4) see relationships to other art forms, such as music, art, drama, sculpture, and so on.

Finally, *in perceiving these elements as aesthetic qualities,* they (1) help children become aware of sensory elements in the environment for their own sake, thus becoming more "sensuously responsive" to their environment; (2) offer alternative ways of expressing ideas, feelings, needs in visual-kinesthetic forms; (3) make children responsive to and easily suggestible to a rich flow of imagery; and (4) provide the means whereby children may make creative transformations from direct experiences into tangible dance forms.

No one element or phenomenon occurs in isolation. Even in enumerating the preceding criteria, we are aware that they do not necessarily follow a sequential order and that they do not necessarily occur that way in children's development. If these criteria serve as broad indicators of growth and change, however, we can perhaps determine whether there are identifiable modes of a child's behavior in dance that point to an evolving style that is uniquely his.

Apart from those factors that are intrinsic to dance, there are generalizable behaviors which children reveal through the very nature of their involvement in the creative process. Such observations offer rich insights not only in relation to a child's response to dance as a specific art form, but in relation to his self-identification in a creative experience. What we are looking to are other personality characteristics which, in varying degrees, are reflected in any creative effort.

1. *Emotional involvement* is evidence from a child that he has the necessary impetus for creative work, demonstrated by his increasing ability to initiate ideas for his own movement explorations; with continued experiences, his involvement reaches an intensity and presence of which he becomes aware.

2. *Focus on a problem* involves concentration in elaborating or refining feelings and impressions in the sense of beginning to structure an idea. It is the initial move to make a form out of the formless; relating new data to existing information leading toward a solution.

3. *Development of an idea into an objective form* which eventually leads to a creative "product" in the sense of an expression shaped by the selected use of movement elements. It is not that the product is of sole importance, but that the process of creating something meaningful for the child must be externalized.

4. *Fulfillment as a result of the release of the imagination.* This aspect of behavior is least easily described. As each child creates dance forms that are uniquely his, he expresses fulfillment in his own idiomatic way (for example, through gestures and facial expressions, but most important, through greater emotional involvement). Finally and always, it rests with the sensitive teacher to observe the qualitative changes in behavior as each child realizes some tangible evidence of his imaginative powers.

VI
Resources

Records for dance accompaniment

British Educational Dance Records for Young Children, "Listen and Move" (eight 45-r.p.m. records; eight compositions for dance with record guide). Time Productions Limited; 260 Deansgate; Manchester 3, England.

Dietrich, Sally Tobin.
    Album I, "Dance and Play" (three 78-r.p.m. records)
    Album II, "Dance and Play" (three 78-r.p.m. records)
    Album III, "Rhythmic Play" (four 78-r.p.m. records)
    Sally Tobin Dietrich; 134 Sherman Avenue; Rockville Center, N.Y.

Gilbert, Pia, "Music for the Modern Dance" (12-inch lp), HLP 4015. Hector Records; 115 Manhattan Ave.; Waldwick, N.J.

James, Phoebe. "Creative Rhythms for Children" (twenty-four 78 r.p.m. records). Children's Music Center; 5373 West Pico Blvd.; Los Angeles, Calif. (Recommended for very young children.)

Miller, Freda. "Records for Dance."
    Album I, "Accompaniment for Technique"
    Album II, "Second Album for Dance"
    Album III, "Third Album for Dance"
    Album IV, "Music for Rhythms and Dance"
    Album V, "Fifth Album for Dance"
    Freda Miller Records for Dance; 131 Bayview Ave.; Northport, N.Y.

Ortmans, Kay.
    "Music for Movement," No. 1 KOP-131
    "Music for Movement," No. a KOP-132
    Kay Ortmans Productions; 2005 Alba Road; Ben Lomond, Calif. (Highly recommended.)

Landrey, Ann. "Dance with Me" (record with book), music by Betty Walberg. James H. Heineman; 60 E. 42nd St.; New York, N.Y.

Perrey, Jean Jacques, and Gershon Kingsley. "The In Sound from Way Out," VRS 9222. (Electronic music.) Vanguard Recording Society; 71 W. 23rd St.; New York, N.Y. 10010.

Walberg, Betty. "Dance-A-Long," FC 7651. Folkways/Scholastic Records; 906 Sylvan Ave.; Englewood Cliffs, N.J. (Highly recommended.)

White, Ruth.
    Vol. 1, "Adventures in Rhythms," CC 623 (three records)
    Vol. 2, "Rhythm Instruments with Folk Music from Many

Lands," CC 614 (three records)
"The Rhythms Hour," CC 615 (three records)
"Play Time Rhythms," CC 618 (three records)
"The Fundamentals of Music for Dancers," CC 609 (three records)
"Motivations for Modern Dance," CC 610 (three records)
"Motifs for Dance Composition," CC 611 (three records)
Ruth White, Rhythms Productions; Cheviot Corporation; Dept. DM; Box 33485; Los Angeles, Calif. (Superb quality; 609, 610, 611 suggested for older children.)
Young People's Records.
"Building a City," 711
"Creepy Crawley Caterpillar," 5019
"The Little Fireman," 615
"My Playful Scarf," 1019
"My Playmate the Wind," 4501
"Train to the Zoo," 706
"What the Lighthouse Sees," 702
"When the Sun Shines," 617
"Who Wants a Ride," 806
"Visit to My Little Friend," 1017
The Greystone Corporation; 100 Sixth Ave.; New York, N.Y. (Recommended for preschool and kindergarten.)

Rhythms and chants

Folkways/Scholastic Records.
"Street Games and Songs of the Children of New York," FC 7005
"Ring Games," FC 7004
"Sounds of My City," FC 7041
Folkways/Scholastic Records; 906 Sylvan Ave.; Englewood Cliffs, N.J.
Jenkins, Ella. "Call and Response," FC 7308. Folkways/Scholastic.
Schwartz, Tony. "1, 2, 3, and a Zing, Zing, Zing," FC 7003. Folkways/Scholastic.

Music with narration for dance accompaniment

Barlin, Ann. "Dance-A-Story," LE 101–108 (four albums with eight records and story books). RCA Victor Records; 155 E. 24th Street; New York, N.Y. (Highly recommended for young children.)

Lohoefer, Evelyn P., and Donald McKayle. "Come and See the Peppermint Tree," DPT 101, Educational Activities, Inc., Freeport, N.Y. (Inventive and unusual content.)

Nelson, Esther, and Bruce Haack.
  "The Way Out Record for Children"
  Vol. 1, "Dance Sing and Listen"
  Vol. 2, "Dance Sing and Listen Again"
  Vol. 3, "Dance Sing and Listen Again and Again"
  Dimension 5; Box 185, Kingsbridge Station; Bronx, N.Y.

Tanner, Virginia. "Come Dance with Me," HLP 3078 (two records with booklet, photos, and materials). Hoctor Records; 115 Manhattan Ave.; Waldwick, N.J. (Highly recommended.)

Folk songs and rhythms

Bailey, Charity. "Music Time with Charity Bailey," FC 307. Folkways/Scholastic Records; 906 Sylvan Ave.; Englewood Cliffs, N.J.; "Sing a Song with Charity Bailey," K 156 (two records). Decca Records; 445 Park Ave.; New York, N.Y. 10022.

Guthrie, Woody. "Songs to Grow On," FC 7010. Folkways/Scholastic.

Hughes, Langston. "Rhythms of the World," FC 7340. Folkways/Scholastic.

Jenkins, Ella.
"Rhythm Games and Songs," FC 7057
"This is Rhythm," FC 7652 (separate book available)
"Rhythms of Childhood," FC 653
"Play Your Instrument and Make a Pretty Sound," FC 7665
"Adventures in Rhythm," FC 8273
"Counting Games and Rhythms for the Little Ones," FC 7056
    Folkways/Scholastic.

Seeger, Pete.
"Birds, Beasts, Bugs, or Little Fishes," FC 7010
"Birds, Beasts, Bugs, or Bigger Fishes," FC 7000
"American Folk Songs for Children," FC 7601
"American Games and Activity Songs for Children," FC 7002
"Songs and Play Times," FC 7521
"American Play Parties," FC 7604
Folkways/Scholastic.

Children's songs and general collections

Bailey, Charity. *Sing a Song with Charity Bailey*. Plymouth Music Co., Inc.; 17 W. 60th St.; New York, N.Y.

Boni, Margaret B., and N. Lloyd. *Fireside Book of Folk Songs*. New York: Simon and Schuster, 1947.

Boni, Margaret B., and N. Lloyd. *Favorite American Songs*. New York: Simon and Schuster, 1956.

Glazer, Tom. *A New Treasury of Folk Songs*. New York: Bantam Books, 1961.

Jenkins, Ella. *This Is Rhythm*. Oak Publications; 701 Seventh Ave.; New York, N.Y.

————. *The Ella Jenkins Song Book for Children*. New York: Oak Publications, 1966.

Landeck, Beatrice. *Songs to Grow On*. New York: Marks-Sloane, 1950.

————. *More Songs to Grow On*. New York: Marks-Sloane, 1954.

————. *Echoes of Africa*. New York: David McKay Co., Inc., 1961.

Lomax, John, and Alan Lomax. *Folk Song, USA*. New York: Signet Books, 1966.

Krugman, Lillian D., and Alice J. Ludwig. *Little Calypsos*. Brooklyn, N.Y.: Carl Van Roy Co., 1955.

Krugman, Lillian D., and Alice J. Ludwig. *Song Tales of the West Indies*. Brooklyn, N.Y.: Carl Van Roy Co., 1964.

Music for Early Childhood (New Music Horizons Series). New York: Silver Burdett Co., 1952.

Seegar, Ruth Crawford. *American Folk Songs for Children*. New York: Doubleday & Company, Inc., 1948.

Siegmeister, Elie. *Treasury of American Folk Songs*. New York: Alfred A. Knopf, Inc., 1943.

Weavers Song Book. New York: Harper & Row, Publishers, 1960.

Winn, Marie. *Fireside Book of Children's Songs*. New York: Simon and Schuster, 1966.

Wilder, Alec. *Lullabies and Night Songs*. New York: Harper & Row, Publishers, 1964.

Yurchenco, Henrietta. *A Fiesta of Folk Songs from Spain and Latin America*. New York: G. P. Putnam's Sons, 1967.

Bibliography of books on dance

Andrews, Gladys. *Creative Rhythmic Movement for Children.* Englewood Cliffs, N.J.: Prentice-Hall, Inc., 1954.

Jaques-Dalcroze, Emile. *Eurythmics, Art, and Education.* New York: A. S. Barnes, 1935.

————. *Rhythm, Music, and Education.* New York: G. P. Putnam's Sons, 1941.

Canner, Norma. *And a Time to Dance.* Boston: Beacon Press, 1968.

Gray, Vera, and R. Percival. *Music, Movement, and Mime.* London: Oxford University Press, 1936.

Hawkins, Alma. *Creating Through Dance.* Englewood Cliffs, N.J.: Prentice-Hall, Inc., 1964.

H'Doubler, Margaret. *Dance, A Creative Experience.* Madison: University of Wisconsin Press, 1957.

Jacobus, Lee A. (ed.). *Aesthetics and the Arts.* New York: McGraw-Hill, 1968, pp. 73–93.

Laban, Rudolph. *Modern Educational Dance.* New York: Frederick A. Praeger, 1968.

Langer, Suzanne K. *Feeling and Form.* New York: Charles Scribner's Sons, 1953.

Martin, John. *Introduction to the Dance.* Brooklyn, N.Y.: Dance Horizons, Inc., 1965.

Mettler, Barbara. *Materials of Dance as a Creative Art Activity.* Tuscon, Ariz.: Mettler Studios, 1960.

Murray, Ruth Lovell. *Dance in Elementary Education.* New York: Harper & Row, Publishers, 1963.

Russell, Joan. *Creative Dance in the Primary School.* New York: Frederick A. Praeger, 1968.

Sheets, Maxine. *The Phenomenonology of Dance.* Madison: University of Wisconsin Press, 1966.

Waterman, Elizabeth. *The Rhythm Book.* New York: A. S. Barnes, 1937.

Films

CHILDREN DANCE Children in classrooms from kindergarten through third grade explore concepts of space, time, and force through improvisations and dance studies. Produced and co-directed by Geraldine Dimondstein and Naima Prevots. 16-mm, b/w, sound; rental $5.50, sale: $80. University of California Extension Media Center; 2223 Shattuck Ave.; Berkeley, Calif. 94720.

CHILDREN DISCOVER THEIR WORLD Young children in the summer program at U.S.C. Idyllwild School of Music and Art are involved in art, dance, and music. 16-mm, b/w, 27″; U.S.C. Idyllwild School of Music and Art, Idyllwild, Calif.

DANCE YOUR OWN WAY A small group of elementary school children dance to ethnic music and rhythms under the guidance of Gertrude Copley Knight. 16-mm, color, sound, 10″; rental: $6, sale: $120. Bailey Films; 6509 De Longpre; Hollywood, Calif. 90028.

LEARNING THROUGH MOVEMENT Produced and directed by Ann and Paul Barlin. As a dance specialist in a public elementary school, Ann Barlin explores movement with children from first through sixth grades. 16-mm, b/w, sound, 32″; rental. $20, sale: $165. S-L Film; 5126 Hartwick St.; Los Angeles, Calif. 90041.

MOVEMENT SPEAKS British Ministry of Education. Young English boys in a mining town explore movement problems under the verbal guidance of the headmaster. 16-mm, b/w, sound, 30″. Department of Audio-Visual Utilization; Wayne State University; Detroit, Michigan.

MOVEMENT IN TIME AND SPACE Part of a BBC series called "Discovery and Experience." Preadolescent girls and boys involved in movement problems. 16-mm, b/w, 30″. Peter M. Rodeck & Co.; 4 W. 16th St.; New York, N.Y.

HAIKU Columbia University students under the direction of dancer and choreographer Jane Dudley create dances based on traditional Japanese poetry. Directed and produced by Leo Hurwitz and Manfred Kirchheimer. 16-mm, sound, 27½″; rental: $8, sale: $135. Center for Mass Communication, Columbia University Press; 440 West 110th St.; New York, N.Y. 10025.

SOUND AND MOVEMENT   Movement improvisations accompanied by sounds of voice, hands, feet, and unconventional musical instruments. Directed by Barbara Mettler. 16-mm, color, sound; rental: $9, sale: $180. Tuscon Creative Dance Center; 3131 N. Cherry Ave.; Tuscon, Ariz.

THE ART OF BODY MOVEMENT   Children, teen-agers, and adults demonstrate creative dance taught by Barbara Mettler. Produced by Will Carbo. 16-mm, b/w, sound, 2 reels: 68″; rental: $30, sale: $350. Tuscon Creative Dance Center.

WHAT IS RHYTHM   Natural rhythms in the environments, rhythms made by movements of people, animals, and objects. Animations which explain beats, accents, phrases are shown simply and directly. 16-mm, color only, 11″. Produced by Bailey-Film Associates; 11559 Santa Monica Blvd.; Los Angeles, Calif. 90025.

Index

Index